M3: Defining Your Mind, Maturity & Movement

A Devotional for Spiritual and Personal Growth

Dr. Mya P. Miller

Dr. Mya P. Miller
Email:
Dr.myamiller@chosenministries.co
Paperback ISBN: 979-8-9993593-0-8
Editor: Abigail L. Gonzalez

Table of Contents

Preface

M3: Defining Your Mind, Maturity, & Movement is more than a devotional—it's a roadmap for **spiritual and personal growth**. It's designed to help you **develop a deeper connection with God**, enhance your **biblical understanding**, and **activate your divine purpose boldly**.

For far too long, many have remained **stuck in hesitation—dreaming but not doing, believing but not stepping forward**. This **70-day journey** invites you to **leave behind stagnation and step into supernatural movement**.

Each day's study will challenge you to:

- **Move in Faith**—trusting God beyond logic, beyond doubt, and comfort zones.
- **Master the Word**—developing biblical wisdom that transforms the way you live, work, and lead.
- **Magnify Your Purpose**—not through passive waiting, but through bold, faith-driven action that amplifies the calling God has placed within you.

Through **scripture, reflection, prayer, and journaling**, you'll not only study the Word but actively **apply it to your life**. By the end of these 70 days, you will walk in **greater faith, clarity, and obedience**, fully equipped to **step into the purpose God has already placed within you**.

The time is now.

No more **second-guessing** or **waiting for the perfect moment—you were CHOSEN for this. Let's begin.**

Dedication

First and foremost, I give all glory and honor to God—the Author of this vision, the One who has guided me through every step, and the Source of my strength, wisdom, and purpose. Without Him, none of this would exist. His grace continues to shape my journey, His presence remains my foundation, and His truth fuels my passion to inspire and uplift others.

To my incredible husband, Stefan, and my beloved son, Denham, **THANK YOU** for your unwavering support, encouragement, and belief in me. Stefan, your words inspire me to step boldly into my God-ordained calling, embrace the gifts He has given me, and walk confidently toward the dreams He has entrusted to my heart. You push me beyond hesitation. You constantly remind me that _with_ faith, nothing is impossible. Denham, your love, joy, and presence inspire me every day. Watching you grow strengthens my faith, deepens my purpose, and reminds me of God's goodness. You both are my greatest blessings, and I am grateful beyond measure.

Now to my mother, my grandmother, my close friend backroom—the ones who love me in real life—and my chosen family: thank you for your prayers, your love, and your unwavering support. You've held me down through every season with truth, loyalty, and intercession. You didn't just see the public wins—you carried me through the private warfare. You've stood in the gap, encouraged me when I was low, and uplifted me when I didn't know how to move forward.

To my brothers: thank you for your quiet strength and covering. To my extended family, aunties, uncles, and cousins: thank you for your wisdom, compassion, and laughter. To my beautiful Mother-in-Love and Father-in-Love: your embrace has been supportive. You welcomed me like your own and covered me with love and encouragement. To my colleagues: thank you for your excellence, partnership, and integrity. You've walked with me as purpose was born, tested, and proven. Each of you helped build the foundation I now stand on, and I thank God for your presence, your prayers, and your love—that's real and lasting.

I pray that this devotional ignites transformation in the life of every believer who embarks on this journey. May it challenge you, stretch you, and deepen your understanding of God's Word. May it inspire you to trust Him fully, chase purpose fearlessly, and walk in faith unapologetically.

This is not just a book—it's an invitation, a divine call to believe, step into action, and embrace the supernatural power of God boldly.

Purpose of This Devotional

This **70-day journey** is designed to **challenge the mind and posture of every believer**, pushing you into deeper intimacy with God and a greater understanding of His Word. This experience will offer thought-provoking biblical insights and practical application, helping believers like yourself grow in faith and deepen your spiritual walk.

Throughout this journey, you will:

✅ **Be stretched beyond surface-level faith**—developing spiritual endurance and wisdom.

✅ **Engage in transformative reflection** that renews the heart and mind.

✅ **Strengthen your biblical foundation** through sound doctrine and practical revelation.

✅ **Navigate life's challenges with scriptural truth**—knowing how to apply God's Word effectively.

✅ **Deepen their understanding of divine purpose** and remain steadfast in faith despite adversity.

This is not just another devotional—it's a spiritual growth experience designed to awaken conviction, activate obedience, and cultivate resilience in every believer.

By the end of these 70 days, you will be more equipped, more confident, and more anchored in your faith, ready to walk stronger in truth, deeper in understanding, and bolder in purpose.

Day 1-8:

The Living Water

Day One: Your Relationship with God Secures Your Assignment

Scripture: James 4:8 (NKJV) *"Draw near to God and He will draw near to you."*

Introduction- Ezekiel could not fulfill his calling without first surrendering to God.

Many believers try **stepping into their purpose without submitting to Christ's authority, but there is no shortcut to divine assignment.**

Surrender Strengthens You in the Image of God!

Ezekiel's **strength did not come from himself—it came from his surrender.** When we obey the voice of God, we can trust His vision. When we trust His vision, we can rest in His presence.

"Son of man, stand on your feet, and I will speak to you."
— Ezekiel 2:1

God **instructed Ezekiel to stand—only after he humbled himself was he fully equipped to walk in his prophetic mission**.

When you surrender to God's leading, He strengthens you to complete your assignment.

Reflection: Have You Fully Surrendered?

- Are you **walking in your assignment**, or avoiding **the process required to be prepared**?
- Do you **trust God fully**, or are you still seeking **comfort over obedience**?
- Are you **drawing near to God**, allowing Him to guide **your calling and purpose**?

Prayer

Lord, I surrender every part of my life to You. Make me more like You, remove distractions, and help my heart stay focused on Your purpose. Help me to trust Your voice, embrace Your vision, and walk confidently in my calling. In Jesus' name, Amen.

Day Two: The Blessing is the Covering, *not* the Compensation

Scripture: Luke 15:17 (NKJV) *"But when he came to himself, he said, 'How many of my father's hired servants have bread enough and to spare, and I perish with hunger!'"*

Introduction- The **parable of the prodigal son** reveals a profound truth....

The real blessing was never the money, possessions, or temporary freedom, but **the father's covering**.

Many seek **compensation**—chasing **wealth, influence, or status**—while missing the **true gift: God's presence, guidance, and protection**.

Leaving the Covering Too Soon- The **prodigal son demanded his inheritance**, thinking it was enough:

"Father, give me the portion of goods that falls to me." — Luke 15:12

The prodigal son left too soon without wisdom, maturity, or accountability. He assumed **possessions would sustain him,** but **his father's presence** was **the true source of provision**.

His decision led to **spiritual hunger, isolation, and desperation**.

Reflection: Are You Seeking Compensation or Covering?

- Are you **chasing temporary gains** or staying **rooted in God's covering**?
- Have you become **spiritually hungry**, lowering your standards?
- Do you need to **return to the presence of the Father**, where true peace exists?

Prayer

Lord, help me recognize that my true blessing is Your covering, not temporary possessions. Keep me anchored in Your presence, and strengthen me to seek You above all else. In Jesus' name, Amen.

Day Three: Returning to the Covering

Scripture: Luke 15:18 (NKJV) *"I will arise and go to my father, and will say to him, 'Father, I have sinned against heaven and before you.'"*

Introduction- The **prodigal son realized his true provision was at home**. He **repented**—not just in **thought**, but in **action**—returning to **his father's covering**.

The greatest victory was not just **his realization**—it was **his return**.

Hunger Creates Crisis

When the son **rejected his covering**, he found himself in a **crisis**:

"And he would gladly have filled his stomach with the pods that the swine ate, and no one gave him anything." — Luke 15:16

Spiritual hunger leads to **compromise**:

- Lowering **standards for temporary gratification.**
- Accepting **connections that weaken faith.**
- Looking for **worldly substitutes instead of returning to God.**

Esau did the same—selling **his birthright for stew,** choosing **momentary satisfaction over eternal inheritance** (Genesis 25:29-34).

Reflection: Are You Returning or Remaining in Lack?

- Have you **forgotten where your true covering lies**?

- Are you **repenting for chasing temporary blessings** over eternal fulfillment?
- Are you **ready to return**, knowing **His grace is waiting**?

Prayer

Lord, I arise and return to You. Let me seek Your presence above all else, trusting that in You I find true provision, peace, and purpose. Do not allow me to lower my standards for temporary gratification; instead, keep my eyes fixed on You. Father, give me strength and wisdom to submit to Your way and Your will, O God. Do not allow me to sell my birthright for worldly desires that are displeasing to You. In Jesus' name, Amen.

Day Four: The Power of Waiting on God

Scripture: Acts 1:4 (NKJV) *"And being assembled together with them, He commanded them not to depart from Jerusalem, but to wait for the Promise of the Father."*

Introduction- Waiting can feel like **a delay**, but it's **often a divine setup**.

In this passage, Jesus commands His disciples to stay in Jerusalem, assuring them that waiting would lead to **supernatural empowerment**.

Many believers struggle with waiting, seeing it as **an obstacle rather than a process**. But Jesus made it clear— before they could **walk in Kingdom authority, they had to first receive divine strength**.

The Purpose of the Wait

Waiting on God **reveals faith, trust, and readiness**. It demonstrates:

- **Trust in God's timing**—Believing His promises come at **the appointed time** (Habakkuk 2:3).
- **Preparation for greater responsibility**—We must **receive before we can pour out** (Isaiah 40:31).
- **Spiritual empowerment**—The Holy Spirit **equips believers** to complete their assignment (John 14:26).

"For John truly baptized with water, but you shall be baptized with the Holy Spirit not many days from now." — Acts 1:5

Reflection: Are You Trusting God's Timing?

- Are you **rushing ahead**, or waiting for **divine revelation**?
- Have you embraced **the process of preparation**, or are you trying to move prematurely?
- Do you believe that waiting is **leading to empowerment, not delay**?

Prayer

Lord, help me embrace patience in this season of waiting. Strengthen me to trust Your timing, knowing that You are preparing me for something greater. Teach me to posture myself with humility and readiness, and to walk through the process that prepares me for my divine destination. Do not allow me to get ahead of Your timing, O God, but help me trust You in all that I do. Align my actions, words, and thoughts with Your will. Empower me to believe in and receive all that You have ordained for me. In Jesus' name, Amen.

Day Five: The Danger of Moving Too Soon

Scripture: Acts 1:8 (NKJV) *"But you shall receive power when the Holy Spirit has come upon you."*

Introduction- Many believers struggle with **impatience**, desiring to **step into elevation without revelation**.

Without spiritual preparation, assignments can become a **burden instead of a blessing**.

If the disciples had **left Jerusalem prematurely**, they would have **missed the outpouring of the Spirit,** rendering them powerless to **fulfill their mission**.

Waiting is not **a setback**—it is **a setup for Kingdom power**.

The Cost of Moving Too Soon

Rushing ahead can lead to:

- **Missed divine appointments**—God's blessings come **in His timing, not ours**.
- **Unprepared assignments**—Without equipping, we may struggle to **handle the weight of our calling**.
- **Spiritual depletion**—Moving forward **without the Holy Spirit** can leave us **weak and discouraged**.

Jesus commanded His disciples to **wait first, then move**, ensuring they were **fully empowered** before stepping into their mission.

Reflection: Are You Moving Too Soon?

- Are you **waiting on God's direction**, or are you moving out of **impatience**?
- Have you allowed **spiritual preparation** to refine you, or are you trying to elevate yourself prematurely?
- Are you willing to **wait for the Spirit's empowerment**, knowing it will strengthen your assignment?

Prayer

Lord, teach me the sacred discipline of waiting. Shape my heart to trust Your divine process and receive the full outpouring of Your Spirit before I take another step. Cultivate unwavering patience within me, O God, and anchor my focus on what You've placed before me. Help me recognize that delay is not denial—it is Your invitation to develop, refine, and become all You've destined me to be. Guard me from distraction and position me to walk with purpose through preparation. Holy Spirit, lead me. Cover me. Empower me. Let every part of my life—my thoughts, my words, my actions—align with Your will. I yield every decision, every desire, and every moment to You. I trust You, Lord. I need You to govern every area of my life with wisdom, clarity, and fire. In Jesus' mighty name, Amen.

Day Six: Embrace Your Wilderness Season

Scripture: Luke 4:1-13 (NKJV) *"Then Jesus, being filled with the Holy Spirit, returned from the Jordan and was led by the Spirit into the wilderness."* — Luke 4:1

Introduction- This passage reveals a critical **truth**—before stepping fully into His assignment, **Jesus was led into the wilderness** by the **Spirit of God**.

It was in **this place of isolation, testing, and fasting** that He was **strengthened for His mission**.

Many believers assume that salvation guarantees ease, yet Scripture shows that accepting the call means preparing for the assignment. Wilderness seasons are not punishments; they are simply training grounds where faith is refined and dependence on God deepens.

Why the Wilderness?

- **It is an ordained season**—Jesus was **led by the Spirit** (Luke 4:1).
- **It is a place of testing**—Satan tempted Jesus **in His most vulnerable state**.
- **It strengthens spiritual endurance**—Jesus fasted **for forty days**, relying **solely on God's power**.

The wilderness **reveals true dependency**—it teaches believers that **supernatural strength comes from surrender**.

Lessons from Jesus' Testing

1. **Satan Tests Your Appetite**
   o The devil tempted Jesus to **turn stones into bread**, appealing to **His physical hunger** (Luke 4:3).
   o Jesus **rejected the offer**, declaring:
   o *"Man shall not live by bread alone, but by every word of God."* — **Luke 4:4 (NKJV)**
   o **Spiritual fulfillment outweighs physical satisfaction**—discipline sustains destiny.
2. **Satan Tests Your Desires**
   o The enemy **offered Jesus power and authority** (Luke 4:6-7).
   o Jesus refused, affirming His commitment to **God alone**:
   o *"You shall worship the Lord your God, and Him only you shall serve."* — **Luke 4:8 (NKJV)**
   o **Satan will test your heart to see if you love God or only what He can do for you.**
3. **Satan Tests Your Trust in God**
   o The devil tried to convince Jesus to **throw Himself down**, daring **God to prove His faithfulness** (Luke 4:9-10).
   o Jesus rebuked him:
   o *"You shall not tempt the Lord your God."* — **Luke 4:12 (NKJV)**
   o **Faith is not reckless—it is surrendered obedience.**

The Power of Fasting and Spiritual Strength

- **Jesus did not eat** during His time in the wilderness.
- He was **filled with the Spirit**, proving that **true sustenance comes from God**.

- **Spiritual battles require spiritual preparation—** natural resources cannot sustain a supernatural calling.

Believers **lose battles because they try to fight spiritual warfare with worldly tactics**.

Reflection: Are You Embracing Your Wilderness Season?

- Are you **trusting the process**, or are you **trying to escape it**?
- Are you **feeding yourself spiritually**, or **relying on external comforts**?
- Are you **standing firm in the Word**, or **falling into the enemy's deception**?

Prayer

Lord, help me to embrace my wilderness season, knowing that You are strengthening me for my assignment. Let me rely fully on Your provision and reject the distractions of the enemy. Teach me to walk in obedience, humility, and power. In Jesus' name, Amen.

Day Seven: What Well Are You Drinking From?

Scripture: John 4:10 (NKJV) *"Jesus answered and said to her, 'If you knew the gift of God, and who it is who says to you, "Give Me a drink," you would have asked Him, and He would have given you living water.'"*

Introduction- Jesus met the **Samaritan woman at the well** in search of **physical water**, but He pointed her toward **a greater source—Living Water**.

Do you find yourself drawing from worldly wells, seeking success, validation, or temporary fulfillment, yet still feeling empty?

Jesus **invites us to drink deeply from Him**, yet some hesitate, standing near the well but never drawing from its life-giving source.

Worldly Wells Leave Us Empty

The world offers many wells, but none truly satisfy:

- **The well of success** promises achievement but lacks lasting peace.
- **The well of relationships** may offer companionship, but cannot replace God's presence.
- **The well of material gain** provides comfort but leaves the soul dry.
- **The well of self-reliance** convinces us we can handle life alone, yet without Christ, we remain spiritually parched.

Reflection: Are You Drawing from the Right Well?

✔ Are you drinking from **temporary wells**, or are you drawing from Christ?

✔ Do you recognize areas where **you've sought fulfillment in things that leave you empty**?

✔ Is **fear** stopping you from fully embracing the **living water Jesus offers**?

Prayer

Lord, expose the empty wells I've clung to—those that cannot nourish, restore, or satisfy my soul. Redirect my thirst toward You, the everlasting fountain of life. Father, I declare that as long as my eyes remain fixed on You, living water will overflow in every area of my life. No drought, no lack, no dry place can remain where Your Spirit dwells. Keep me deeply rooted and unwaveringly connected to You, for in Your presence there is fullness, flow, and fruitfulness. Let my wellspring be Your Word—alive, active, and abundant within me. Cover me, lead me, and saturate me with divine clarity and power. In Jesus' mighty name, Amen.

Day Eight: The Gift of Living Water

Scripture: John 6:35 (NKJV) *"Jesus said to them, 'I am the bread of life. He who comes to Me shall never hunger, and he who believes in Me shall never thirst.'"*

The Gift That Satisfies

Jesus **reminds us** that true fulfillment comes only from Him. If we truly understood **the gift of God**, our lives would be transformed:

- **Our days would be enriched** with **purpose and direction** (*Psalm 37:23*).
- **Our prayers would be strengthened** by intimacy with the Father (*James 5:16*).
- **Our vision would be clarified**, seeing life through the lens of faith (*Proverbs 3:5-6*).

To **drink deeply from Christ** is to receive **wisdom, peace, and renewal** that never runs dry.

A Call to Examine Your Source

Jesus offers **living water**, yet some still **hesitate** to receive it fully. Today, ask yourself:

✔ Am I trying to satisfy my thirst with **temporary things**?

✔ Am I willing to **trust Jesus to be my source** in every area of life?

✔ How can I **commit to drinking deeply from His presence** every day?

Prayer

Lord, I surrender every false source I've clung to and receive the fullness of Your living water. Refresh me. Renew me. Saturate my heart with Your divine presence. Align my heart with Your will. Sharpen my ears to hear Your voice clearly, and grant me revelation, wisdom, and understanding for this season. Deliver me from every spirit of fear and frustration, and empower me to trust You like never before. Father, I thank You for the privilege to serve You. I thank You that You will use me today as a vessel to bear witness of Your greatness and power. I bind every lie of the enemy and cast it back to the pit of hell. I shall not fall prey to his deception, confusion, or distraction. I walk in victory. I walk in truth. I walk in the power of Your Spirit. In Jesus' mighty name, Amen.

Day 9-19:

The Exposure of Influence

Day Nine: God is Exposing and Opposing the Enemy

Scripture: 2 Samuel 1:1-14 (NKJV) *"So David said to him, 'How was it you were not afraid to put forth your hand to destroy the Lord's anointed?'"* — 2 Samuel 1:14

Introduction- This passage reveals a moment of divine exposure and elevation.

King Saul and his army fell, marking the end of his reign. During grief, an Amalekite, driven by greed and deception, sees an opportunity to manipulate the situation for personal gain. God is at work, uncovering hidden motives, dealing with the enemy, and positioning David for his next season.

The Consequences of Falsehood

The Amalekite wrongly assumed that delivering Saul's crown and jewelry to David would grant him favor. He underestimated the character of a true servant of God.

David did not celebrate Saul's demise—he honored God's anointing, refusing to act out of bitterness. The Amalekite's deception led to his destruction, proving that God will always expose what is hidden.

"How was it you were not afraid to put forth your hand to destroy the Lord's anointed?" — 2 Samuel 1:14

David understood a critical truth:

"Beloved, do not avenge yourselves, but rather give place to wrath; for it is written, 'Vengeance is Mine, I will repay,' says the Lord." — Romans 12:19

Rather than retaliate, David chose reverence and restraint, trusting God's justice instead of taking matters into his own hands.

Reflection: Where is God Revealing Truth in Your Life?

Are you trying to manipulate a situation instead of trusting God's timing?

Are you allowing God to uncover truth and expose deception in your life?

Are there moments you've wanted to take control instead of trusting God's justice?

Prayer

Lord, help me surrender my battles to You. Reveal any deception, guide me in wisdom, and strengthen me to walk in faith, trusting Your justice over my own. In Jesus' name, Amen.

Day Ten: Trusting God's Process for Elevation

Scripture: Exodus 14:14 (NKJV) *"The LORD will fight for you, and you shall hold your peace."*

Lessons for the Believer

This passage teaches three key spiritual principles.

God will expose deception. The Amalekite thought his lie would elevate him, but God revealed the truth (Luke 8:17). Honor God's timing. David had chances to eliminate Saul but waited on God's plan, not revenge (Ecclesiastes 3:1). Keep your eyes on God even in sorrow; David stayed focused on his purpose, trusting God for elevation (Psalm 34:17-18).

A Call to Trust God's Process

When confronted with opportunities or information, believers must ask: Is this aligned with God's will? What is the hidden motive behind this?

David's story reminds us that our emotions should never dictate our destiny.

God is working behind the scenes, exposing deception, revealing truth, and positioning His people for elevation.

Reflection: Are You Trusting God to Elevate You?

Are there hidden motives in your life that need exposure? Are you allowing God to reveal what must be removed? Are you patiently trusting God's process instead of forcing your own?

Stay faithful—what God reveals, He will also redeem. Your next season is coming.

Prayer

Lord, help me to trust Your process for elevation. Reveal anything in my life that does not align with Your will and give me discernment to walk in integrity and faith. I surrender my journey to You, knowing You will position me for greater things. In Jesus' name, Amen.

Day Eleven: Boldness Through Christ

Scripture: Acts 4:13 (NKJV) *"Now when they saw the boldness of Peter and John, and perceived that they were uneducated and untrained men, they marveled. And they realized that they had been with Jesus."*

Introduction- Peter and John stood **boldly in the temple**, preaching the gospel before the priests and religious leaders. Their words challenged tradition and **declared the resurrection of Jesus**, something the religious establishment refused to accept.

Not only did they proclaim the truth, but they also **performed a miraculous healing**, restoring a man who had been crippled for 41 years (Acts 3:2-10). The rulers and elders couldn't **deny the power behind the miracle**, but they sought to **intimidate and silence** Peter and John.

Opposition Cannot Silence God's Power

The religious leaders asked, *"By what power or by what name have you done this?"* (Acts 4:7). They recognized authority in the name of Jesus but refused to submit to it.

Filled with the **Holy Spirit**, Peter boldly declared: *"Let it be known to you all, and to all the people of Israel, that by the name of Jesus Christ of Nazareth, whom you crucified, whom God raised from the dead, by Him this man stands here before you whole."* — Acts 4:10 (NKJV)

Despite opposition, **Peter and John remained firm**, knowing that the presence of God **was evident in their lives**.

Reflection: Do You Stand Boldly in Christ?

- Are you willing to **speak the truth even when faced with resistance**?
- Do you find **confidence in God, or do you seek approval from the world**?
- How can you **deepen your faith** so that it remains unwavering in challenging times?

Prayer

Lord, strengthen me to stand boldly in my faith. When opposition comes, let me remain steadfast in Your truth. Fill me with confidence in Your power and presence. In Jesus' name, Amen.

Day Twelve: The Evidence of Being with Jesus

Scripture: Acts 4:13 (NKJV) *"Now when they saw the boldness of Peter and John, and perceived that they were uneducated and untrained men, they marveled. And they realized that they had been with Jesus."*

What Does it Mean to Be with Jesus?

Peter and John's **boldness, wisdom, and spiritual authority** did not come from **earthly credentials**—they came from their **relationship with Jesus**.

When you **spend time with the Lord**, your life changes. You develop:

- **Unshakable faith**—Trusting God in every circumstance (Proverbs 3:5-6).
- **Spiritual boldness**—Declaring His truth, even in the face of opposition (2 Timothy 1:7).
- **Kingdom authority**—Moving in power, wisdom, and discernment (Luke 10:19).
- **Unwavering obedience**—Following His Word no matter the cost (John 14:15).

Peter and John didn't need **human validation**—they operated in **spiritual authority**, proving that **God's presence cannot be hidden**.

Standing Boldly in Christ

As believers, we will always face **challenges** when we stand boldly in faith.

Some will question, intimidate, or try to silence the truth. But as Peter and John did, **we must remain steadfast, knowing that God is with us**.

"If God is for us, who can be against us?" — Romans 8:31 (NKJV)

Instead of seeking **approval from the world**, we must commit to **standing on the truth of Scripture**.

Reflection: How Will You Show You Have Been With Jesus?

- Do your **actions and words reflect your time with God**?
- Are you **walking in Kingdom authority** rather than relying on human credentials?
- How can you **grow closer to Jesus so that His presence is undeniable in your life**?

Prayer

Lord, help me to walk boldly in my faith. Let my life reflect Your presence, and may I stand unshaken in Your truth. Strengthen me to follow Your Word, even when faced with opposition. In Jesus' name, Amen.

Day Thirteen: Who Has Your Influence in This Hour?

Scripture: Jeremiah 28:15 (NKJV) *"Then the prophet Jeremiah said to Hananiah the prophet, 'Hear now, Hananiah, the LORD has not sent you, but you make this people trust in a lie.'"*

Introduction- Jeremiah was called to deliver an **unpopular** message, warning the people of impending judgment due to their **sin and disobedience**.

Despite repeated warnings, they **refused to listen**:

"If you will not listen to Me, to walk in My law which I have set before you... then I will make this house like Shiloh, and I will make this city a curse to all the nations of the earth."
— Jeremiah 26:4-6

Jeremiah **stood alone, proclaiming truth** while false prophets sought to **silence him** and distort God's message.

Deception vs. Divine Truth

Hananiah, a **false prophet**, boldly contradicted Jeremiah, claiming that God would soon break **the yoke of Babylon** and restore the people within two years. To **prove his claim**, he physically broke the wooden yoke from Jeremiah's neck.

Yet, **deception cannot stand against divine truth**. God **always exposes falsehoods**:

"For false christs and false prophets will rise and show signs and wonders to deceive, if possible, even the elect."
— Mark 13:22

Hananiah preached **comfort rather than correction**, but Jeremiah remained faithful. He understood that whether the people **accepted it or not, God's word would come to pass**.

Reflection: Are You Guarding Your Influence?

- Are you **being swayed by words that sound good but contradict God's truth**?
- Do you seek **spiritual correction**, or do you only accept comfortable messages?
- Have you allowed **emotion or urgency to dictate decisions instead of God's wisdom**?

Prayer

Lord, help me recognize deception and trust Your truth. Give me discernment to know what is truly from You, and strengthen me to stand firm. In Jesus' name, Amen.

Day Fourteen: Guarding Your Influence and Trusting God's Plan

Scripture: Isaiah 40:8 (NKJV) *"The grass withers, the flower fades, but the word of our God stands forever."*

Lessons for the Believer

Jeremiah's experience teaches several critical lessons:

- **Be Discerning About Who You Listen To** – Not everyone who claims to speak for God is truly sent by Him (1 John 4:1).
- **God's Truth Is Not Always Comfortable** – Hananiah preached relief, but Jeremiah preached refinement. Sometimes, **God calls us to endure rather than escape**.
- **Opposition Does Not Cancel God's Plan** – Jeremiah stood firm despite **intimidation, isolation, and hostility**.

A Call to Guard Your Influence

Who has your **ear** in this season?

Whose **words** shape your decisions, emotions, and faith?

False influences come when **circumstances are fragile**— during tragedy, uncertainty, or when emotions run high. In those moments, we must **anchor ourselves in God's Word**, ensuring that **His voice is louder than all others**.

Jeremiah refused to **compromise truth**, reminding us that **God's word will always stand**—no matter what others say:

"The LORD will fight for you, and you shall hold your peace." — Exodus 14:14

Reflection: Who Has Your Influence?

- Are you seeking **God's correction or simply comforting words**?
- Are you **discerning about who speaks into your life**?
- How can you **ensure that God's voice carries the most weight in your decisions**?

Prayer

Lord, let Your voice be the loudest influence in my life. Help me seek correction, not just comfort, and walk faithfully in Your truth. In Jesus' name, Amen.

Day Fifteen: Beware of the Hireling

Scripture: John 10:12 (NKJV) *"But a hireling, he who is not the shepherd, one who does not own the sheep, sees the wolf coming and leaves the sheep and flees; and the wolf catches the sheep and scatters them."*

Introduction- Jesus warns that **hirelings don't care for the sheep**—they operate **in title but not in truth**, motivated by **self-interest** rather than **the heart of Christ**.

The Pharisees **rejected Jesus** because His teachings **disrupted their traditions and challenged their influence**. They prioritized **their authority over the people's well-being**.

Discerning Leadership in Your Life

We must **be mindful of who we follow**, because **the wrong leadership can push us toward destiny or destruction**.

Some **spiritual influences** today prioritize:

- **Influence over transformation**
- **Comfort over correction**
- **Personal gain over God's purpose**

Jesus calls us to **recognize leadership that operates under His truth, not selfish ambition**.

Reflection: Are You Following a Hireling?

- Are you **placing trust in leaders who prioritize influence over faithfulness**?

- Do you **follow guidance that aligns with God's Word**, or messages that simply feel good?
- How can you **ensure your heart remains aligned with Christ's truth**?

Prayer

Lord, help me discern true leadership. Remove every false influence and every wolf in sheep's clothing that seeks to distract or deceive me. Lead me into truth, transformation, and complete obedience to Your will. Father, grant me divine wisdom and teach me to yield to the guidance of the Holy Spirit. Shield me from every trap of Satan and silence every lie of deception that tries to cloud my vision. Do not let me fall into the spirit of religion, but instead, fill me with the Spirit of Truth—pure, powerful, and active in every area of my life. Deliver me from the comfort of compromise and the contamination of complacency. Empower me to trust Your blueprint and fully walk in the purpose You established for me. Keep me close to You, O Lord. Do not allow me to be misled or drawn into destruction. Let every step I take be rooted in Your truth and covered by Your grace. In Jesus' mighty name, Amen.

Day Sixteen: Recognizing the Good Shepherd

Scripture: John 10:11 (NKJV) *"I am the good shepherd. The good shepherd gives His life for the sheep."*

Introduction- Jesus presents Himself as the **Good Shepherd**, the one who **watches over, protects, and nurtures** His sheep.

Unlike a hireling, He **sacrifices His life** rather than abandoning His flock.

Jesus declares that **true believers recognize His voice and follow Him,** while **those who serve themselves flee when challenges arise**.

Knowing the Voice of the Good Shepherd

Jesus makes it clear that His sheep **know His voice** and will not follow a stranger:

"But he who enters by the door is the shepherd of the sheep. To him the doorkeeper opens, and the sheep hear his voice; and he calls his own sheep by name and leads them out." — John 10:2-3

A true believer **hears, recognizes, and submits** to Christ's leadership.

But **many unknowingly follow voices** that **offer comfort, not correction, influence, but not transformation**.

Reflection: Who Are You Following?

- Have you **fully surrendered to Christ** as your Good Shepherd?

- Are you **following voices that challenge your faith, or ones that make you comfortable**?
- What steps can you take to **strengthen your ability to hear and follow God's voice**?

Prayer

Lord, help me discern Your voice above all others. Lead me in wisdom, strengthen my faith, and remove anything that hinders my obedience to You. In Jesus' name, Amen.

Day Seventeen: The Danger of Hardening Your Heart

Scripture: Exodus 8:1-2 (NKJV) *"Thus says the Lord: 'Let My people go, that they may serve Me. But if you refuse to let them go, behold, I will smite all your territory with frogs.'"*

Introduction- Pharaoh's refusal to **release God's people** wasn't just **stubbornness**—it was **defiance against the living God**.

Through **ten plagues**, God **displayed His power**, revealing that no earthly ruler could stand against Him.

When God **steps into a battle**, He does not **negotiate**—He **declares His will with absolute authority**:

"Thus says the Lord: 'Let My people go, that they may serve Me.'" — Exodus 8:1

God allowed Pharaoh **to obey**, but his hardened heart led him into **a confrontation with the Almighty**.

The Danger of Hardening Your Heart

Pharaoh's resistance serves as a warning:

"But Pharaoh hardened his heart at this time also; neither would he let the people go." — Exodus 8:32

A hardened heart causes:

- **Spiritual blindness**—rejecting God's will even when His presence is evident (Hebrews 3:8).

- **Destruction**—choosing disobedience leads to consequences beyond what we can bear (Proverbs 16:18).
- **Divine opposition**—when we fight against God, we will never prevail (Acts 5:39).

Pharaoh rejected **nine warnings** to yield to God and His Word. His pride led to **devastation, loss, and destruction**.

Reflection: Is Your Heart Hardened Toward God?

- Are you **rejecting His instruction** due to pride or resistance?
- Has God been **giving you warnings**, but you have ignored them?
- How can you **soften your heart and yield to His will**?

Prayer

Lord, remove any hardness in my heart that keeps me from fully submitting to Your will. Help me to trust and obey, knowing that Your plans lead to life and restoration. In Jesus' name, Amen.

Day Eighteen: Trusting God Over Worldly Idols

Scripture: Psalm 20:7 (NKJV) *"Some trust in chariots, and some in horses; But we will remember the name of the Lord our God."*

Introduction- Pharaoh and his magicians **attempted to replicate God's signs**, but they could not **control the outcome**. Even Satan's power is **limited** when confronted by the **authority of God**.

"Then the magicians said to Pharaoh, 'This is the finger of God.'" — Exodus 8:19

God **used Egypt's false gods** to **break their pride**, turning their sacred things into **curses** to expose their misplaced worship.

Who Are You Trusting?

Like Pharaoh, many today place their trust in **worldly idols**—power, money, status, traditions, and even false spirituality. Some **turn to horoscopes, crystals, or self-reliance**, trying to control their destiny.

But no earthly power can **override God's sovereignty**:

"You shall have no other gods before Me." — Exodus 20:3

It's **dangerous** to **tussle with God**, yet many do so by **rejecting His voice, resisting His will, and refusing His calling**.

Reflection: Are You Submitting or Resisting God?

- Are you **placing trust in temporary things** instead of the **true and living God**?
- Have you **ignored His warnings**, assuming you can handle things in your own strength?
- Is your heart **fully surrendered to His plan**?

Prayer

Lord, I surrender my idols, distractions, and self-reliance to You. Help me to trust in Your authority, knowing that only You can lead me into purpose and truth. In Jesus' name, Amen.

Day Nineteen: Guarding Your House from Wrong Influences

Scripture: Isaiah 39:3 (NKJV) *"Then Isaiah the prophet went to King Hezekiah, and said to him, 'What did these men say, and from where did they come to you?'"*

Introduction- King Hezekiah **entertained a dangerous visit** from the Babylonians, failing to recognize **their true motives.**

Though previously **near death and granted more years,** he **misused his extended time** by exposing **his treasures to the wrong people.**

We must ask ourselves: **Are we allowing access to people who will strengthen our purpose or sabotage it?**

Discern Who You Allow in Your Life

- **Hezekiah failed to realize Babylon's motives,** welcoming **an enemy disguised as a friend** (Isaiah 39:2).
- **Not everyone who celebrates you is for you**—some come to **observe, not uplift**.
- **Before opening doors**, seek God's wisdom.

Reflection: Are You Protecting Your House?

- Are you **discerning relationships,** or allowing **convenience to dictate connections**?
- Are you **humble in your blessings,** or exposing **too much for personal validation**?
- Are your **alignments pushing you toward destiny,** or pulling you into **destruction**?

Prayer

Lord, grant me the wisdom to discern who I allow into my life. Keep me anchored in humility, ensuring that my blessings glorify You. Teach me to protect what You've given me, ensuring that every connection aligns with Your purpose. In Jesus' name, Amen.

Day 20-22:

The Betrayal

Day Twenty: Betrayal Does Not Cancel Prophecy

Scripture: Mark 14:18 (NKJV) *"Assuredly, I say to you, one of you who eats with Me will betray Me."*

Introduction- Jesus knew betrayal was imminent, yet He still **sat among His disciples**, breaking bread with His enemy and continuing His assignment.

Imagine walking with someone for **three years**, only to discover they would betray you **for 30 shekels**. Judas **gave up eternity for a temporary gain**, a reminder that many betray Christ **for far less even today**.

Handling Betrayal with Purpose

Instead of reacting emotionally, Jesus remained **calm**, prepared His disciples, and stayed **focused on His mission**:

"Then He came and found them sleeping, and said to Peter, 'Simon, are you sleeping? Could you not watch one hour?'" — Mark 14:37

Even in **agony**, Jesus pressed forward through **prayer and obedience** to the Father.

Lessons for the Believer

1. **Betrayal Does Not Cancel Prophecy** – Even when faced with hurt, rejection, or disappointment, God's plan **will still come to pass** (Romans 8:28).
2. **Guard Your Heart Against Bitterness** – Hatred **gives hell access to your soul** (Ephesians 4:31).
3. **What You Chase Can Either Kill or Keep You** – Judas **chased money**, leading to his demise (Acts 1:18).

Judas **sat with the anointing, ate with the anointing, and still betrayed the anointing**. His story ended in **tragedy** because when we **align with the enemy**, we lose **access to the Kingdom**.

Reflection: How Do You Respond to Betrayal?

- Are you **letting hurt turn into hatred**, or trusting God to handle the situation?
- Are you **focused on your divine assignment** or distracted by temporary things?
- When faced with adversity, **do you retaliate, or do you turn to prayer and fasting**?

Prayer

Lord, help me stay faithful to my assignment, even in the midst of betrayal. Strengthen me to trust Your plan rather than respond with bitterness. Keep my heart aligned with Your purpose, knowing that all things work together for good. In Jesus' name, Amen.

Day Twenty-One: The Prophecy Will Still Take Place in the Midst of Betrayal

Scripture: Mark 14:10-11, 17-21, 32-50 (NKJV), *"Then Judas Iscariot, one of the twelve, went to the chief priests to betray Him to them."*— Mark 14:10

Introduction- In this passage, we witness **a painful prophecy**—one that had to be fulfilled, even at the expense of the Holy One.

Jesus sat among His disciples, those He had **ministered to, taught, and loved**, and spoke a prophetic word:

"Assuredly, I say to you, one of you who eats with Me will betray Me." (Mark 14:18)

Despite walking with Him for years, **one among them— Judas—had already decided to betray Him for thirty shekels**. His heart had hardened beyond repentance, and his **greed overshadowed his destiny**.

Yet Jesus did not allow betrayal to distract Him. **He remained focused, faithful, and firm in His assignment.** He broke bread with His betrayer, washed his feet, and moved forward, knowing that **prophecy had to be fulfilled**.

Betrayal Does Not Cancel Purpose

Pain **does not stop prophecy**. Betrayal **does not cancel an assignment**.

Jesus understood that **His purpose was greater than His pain**. In moments of betrayal, we must remember:

- **People may fail us, but God's plan does not.**
- **The enemy may plot against us, but our destiny remains secure.**
- **Pain may feel unbearable, but God's promise is still in motion.**

Judas **chased wealth**, and it led to his destruction. **Jesus chased His assignment**, and it led to eternal glory.

Reflection: How Do You Handle Betrayal?

- Do you allow **hurt to develop hatred**?
- Do you **trust God's plan**, even when people fail you?
- Are you chasing **God's purpose**, or chasing things that will ultimately destroy you?

Prayer

Father, in moments of betrayal, help me remain focused on Your plan. Guard my heart against resentment and strengthen my spirit to endure trials without wavering in obedience. Teach me to trust that no attack can stop the prophecy You have spoken over my life. Let me chase after You with steadfast faith, refusing to be consumed by the distractions of the enemy. May I walk with integrity, stand in purpose, and remain faithful to Your call. In Jesus' name, Amen.

Day Twenty-Two: Jesus' Response to Betrayal

Scripture: Mark 14:32 (NKJV) *"Then they came to a place which was named Gethsemane; and He said to His disciples, 'Sit here while I pray.'"*

Introduction- Jesus' response to betrayal was **not anger, but prayer**. Rather than **retaliate**, He turned to **fasting, surrendering, and trusting in God's greater plan**.

Even while His disciples **slept**, He pressed through **agony and obedience**, knowing **His mission was greater than His pain**.

Trusting God Over Temporary Pain

Many struggle with **betrayal**, allowing hurt to **turn into resentment**. But Jesus' example reveals a **higher path**:

1. **Prayer Positions You for Purpose** – Jesus didn't dwell in disappointment—He **prayed through it**.
2. **Surrender Brings Peace** – Even in anguish, He trusted **the Father's plan**.
3. **Obedience Strengthens You** – He did **not allow betrayal** to weaken His faith—He pressed deeper into **His divine assignment**.

Reflection: Are You Trusting God in the Midst of Betrayal?

- Are you **staying rooted in prayer**, or reacting out of emotion?
- Do you trust **God's plan over your pain**, knowing He is working everything out?
- Are you **choosing surrender over retaliation**?

Prayer

Lord, let Your example of faithfulness guide me. Keep me steadfast in prayer, trusting Your plan above my emotions. Strengthen me to surrender fully, knowing You are always in control. Keep me from responding to challenges out of my flesh, and help me answer from my character instead. Father develop patience, wisdom, knowledge, and understanding within me. Let wisdom follow me all my days and in all my ways. In Jesus' Mighty, Matchless Name, Amen.

Day 23-30:

The Separation for Action

Day Twenty-Three: Laying Down Your Life for Christ

Scripture: Luke 9:23 (NKJV) *"Then He said to them all, 'If anyone desires to come after Me, let him deny himself, and take up his cross daily, and follow Me.'"*

Introduction- Following Jesus **is not convenient**—it **requires surrender**. To be **true disciples**, we must lay down our **lives, desires, and personal ambitions** to prioritize Him above all else.

What It Means to Lay Down Your Life

To follow Jesus fully, we must be willing to:

- **Prioritize the needs of others** above our own (Philippians 2:3-4).
- **Serve with humility** (Matthew 20:26-28).
- **Sacrifice our time and resources** for Kingdom work (Romans 12:1).
- **Embrace discomfort in obedience to God** (Luke 9:23).

True discipleship is **not about convenience**—it's about **commitment, transformation, and eternal fulfillment**.

Reflection: Are You Willing to Surrender?

- Have you truly **given your life to Christ** in full obedience?

- Are you **willing to embrace sacrifice and discomfort in pursuit of His will**?
- What actions can you take today to **deepen your surrender**?

Prayer

Lord, help me to lay down my life for You. Strengthen me to follow Your will, embrace obedience, and trust You fully. I desire to accommodate You in every area of my life. Help me to manage my time, mind, and resources with intention. I desire to remain committed to serving You and Your Kingdom. Remove any distractions from my life permanently, so I can fully focus on You and what You have entrusted to me in this season. I desire to become the best version of myself. In Jesus' name, Amen.

Day Twenty-Four: Separation for Divine Elevation

Scripture: Genesis 12:1 (NKJV) *"Now the LORD had said to Abram: 'Get out of your country, from your family and from your father's house, to a land that I will show you.'"*

Introduction- God instructed Abram to **separate from his family**, yet he **took Lot with him** (Genesis 12:1-4). This **partial obedience** created unnecessary burdens.

Some **people and places must be removed** for us to walk in divine elevation.

Listening to God's Full Instructions

Abram's journey teaches us:

- **Delayed obedience is disobedience** – Moving **halfway in obedience** can create **unavoidable struggles**.
- **Some separations are necessary** – Lot's presence **caused tension**, but when he left, God **expanded Abram's territory** (Genesis 13:14-15).
- **God's plan requires trust** – Abram did not **know the full destination**, but he **trusted God's direction**.

Reflection: Are You Holding Onto What God Told You to Release?

- Are you **hesitant to let go of people or places** that no longer align with your calling?
- Have you **embraced full obedience**, or are you **only partially following God's instructions**?

- Do you trust that **separation leads to elevation** in your faith journey?

Prayer

Lord, grant me divine wisdom to release anything that no longer aligns with Your plan for my life. Help me walk in full obedience, knowing that every act of surrender positions me for elevation. Father, tune my ear to hear Your voice with clarity and conviction. Prepare me for this new season, and enlarge my capacity—expand my thoughts, my relationships, and my territory—as You take me to greater heights in Your purpose. Empower me to be a light, influencing others to trust, believe, and experience Your goodness. Let my life be a living testimony that invites others to taste and see that You are good. Keep my heart in a posture of gratitude and reverence in this hour. I thank You, Lord, not just for what You've done, but for what You're about to do. In Jesus' mighty name, Amen.

Day Twenty-Five: Breaking Free from Tradition

Scripture: Mark 3:5 (NKJV) *"Then He said to the man, 'Stretch out your hand.' And he stretched it out, and his hand was restored as whole as the other."*

Introduction- Jesus **challenged religious tradition**, choosing to **heal a man** on the Sabbath. The Pharisees were **focused on rules**, while Jesus was **focused on restoration**.

Many believers **miss divine moments** because they **cling to tradition rather than transformation**.

Faith requires **action**—when the **Spirit moves**, we must be **ready to respond**.

The Danger of Prioritizing Tradition Over Transformation

- The Pharisees **knew Jesus could heal**, but they wanted to **discredit His authority** (Mark 3:2).
- Instead of **celebrating the miracle**, they were **focused on legalism**.
- Tradition **kept them bound**, causing them to **miss the breakthrough** right in front of them.

Reflection: Are You Missing Your Moment?

- Are you **waiting for the perfect opportunity**, or **moving when God speaks**?
- Is **tradition blocking your faith**?
- Are you boldly **responding**, or letting **fear and doubt hold you back**?

Prayer

Lord, open my heart to recognize my moment of breakthrough. Let me move when You speak—without hesitation or fear. Remove every distraction and tradition that keeps me from fully surrendering to You. Do not let me operate in the spirit of religion or walk in the behavior of a Pharisee. Instead, Father, allow me to function as a faith-filled believer, fully ready to receive all that You have for me, in whatever way You choose to give it. Do not let my flesh blind my spirit. May my flesh be brought into full submission under Your Word, oh God. I desire to operate in the fullness of Your power and anointing. In Jesus' Mighty Name, Amen.

Day Twenty-Six: Separating from Distractions to Walk in Purpose

Scripture: Acts 16:6 (NKJV) *"Now when they had gone through Phrygia and the region of Galatia, they were forbidden by the Holy Spirit to preach the word in Asia."*

Introduction- Paul's missionary journey required **obedience and separation**.

His **disagreement with Barnabas** led to a **necessary transition**, ensuring he was **aligned with the right partnerships for his next assignment**.

Sometimes, **purpose requires painful separation**.

Lessons from Paul's Journey

- **Some assignments require solitude and new partnerships**—not everyone **can go with you**.
- **Paul separated from Barnabas**, recognizing that **the disagreement was a sign to move forward**.
- **God's "No" leads to a greater "Yes"**—the Macedonia mission was **far more impactful than what Paul originally envisioned**.

Some believers **settle for small victories** because they refuse to **wait for divine assignments**.

Reflection: Are Your Relationships Supporting or Hindering Your Purpose?

- Are you **allowing distractions to delay your assignment**?
- Have you released **relationships that God has told you to step away from**?

- Are you **trusting that separation leads to elevation**?

Prayer

Lord, strengthen me to walk in obedience, even when it requires separation. Teach me to release distractions and embrace divine direction. Let me trust Your wisdom, knowing that every change is part of Your greater plan. In Jesus' name, Amen.

Day Twenty-Seven: Activating Your Faith Through Action

Scripture: James 2:26 (NKJV) *"Faith without works is dead."*

Introduction- Jesus did not just **challenge tradition**—He **called for action**. When He told the man to **stretch out his hand**, the man **obeyed immediately**, activating his healing.

Faith **is not passive**—it requires **obedience, boldness, and action**.

Examples of Unwavering Faith

- **The Woman with the Issue of Blood**—She **pressed through the crowd**, refusing to **miss her moment** (Luke 8:43-44).
- **The Canaanite Woman**—She **didn't care about status**—she begged for **her daughter's healing** (Matthew 15:26-28).

Both **stepped beyond tradition** and into **bold faith**, receiving **their breakthrough**.

Lessons from the Man with the Withered Hand

1. **Faith Requires Agreement with the Spirit** – He didn't hesitate—he **obeyed immediately** (Mark 3:5).
2. **Breakthrough Requires Action** – **Stretching out his hand** was an act of faith that **released his healing**.
3. **Don't Let Fear Stop You** – Many people **sit in church every week** but **refuse to surrender due to fear or shame**.

Reflection: Are You Responding or Hesitating?

- Are you **boldly stepping into faith**, or **waiting for external validation**?
- Have you **acted on God's instruction**, or are you **waiting too long**?
- Are you **letting doubt hold you back**, or choosing to **activate faith**?

Prayer

Lord, help me to activate faith through action. Teach me to listen and respond, trusting that You have already gone before me and paved the way for my success. Develop me to stand in full agreement with Your Spirit, O God, and allow me to stretch my faith in such a way that it moves others to obedience. Father, I desire to fully surrender my mind, heart, ways, and mouth to You. You are the Chief Authority in my life, and I long to be guided by You. So have Your way, and do whatever You need to do in me and through me, O God. It is in Your Son's precious, holy name—Jesus Christ, my Lord and Savior—I pray this prayer. Amen.

Day Twenty-Eight: Transformation Requires Action

Scripture: John 4:28-29 (NKJV) *"The woman then left her waterpot, went her way into the city, and said to the men, 'Come, see a Man who told me all things that I ever did. Could this be the Christ?'"*

Introduction- The Samaritan woman **did not just encounter Jesus**—she **allowed the encounter to change her.**

She came **burdened** but left **bold.** Her **past no longer defined her future**.

Why Do We Settle in Brokenness?

Some believers operate in **spiritual hunger**, content to remain in **struggles rather than transformation**. Like the Samaritan woman:

- Some **hide their wounds**, pretending **pain doesn't exist.**
- Some **avoid deep spiritual encounters**, fearing **exposure**.
- Some **believe their past disqualifies them** from God's grace.

But Jesus meets us **where we are, not to leave us there, but to lift us into freedom**.

Reflection: Are You Stuck or Stepping Into Transformation?

- Are you **willing to move beyond your past**, embracing Christ fully?

- Are you **running from your calling**, or stepping boldly into it?
- Have you **met Jesus**, but failed to allow Him to **transform your life**?

Prayer

Lord, let me no longer settle in brokenness—help me step boldly into the renewal You offer. Teach me to walk beyond my past, ensuring that Your truth defines my future. In Jesus' name, Amen.

Day Twenty-Nine: Cleaning Your Spiritual Temple

Scripture: Matthew 21:12 (NKJV) *"Then Jesus went into the temple of God and drove out all those who bought and sold in the temple, and overturned the tables of the money changers."*

Introduction- Jesus **cleansed the temple**, exposing corruption and **restoring holiness** to God's house. The **temple was designed for worship**, but worldly influences **polluted its purpose**.

Many **struggle with spiritual distractions**, allowing **compromise to weaken their faith**. God calls us to purify our hearts, ensuring our lives reflect true holiness.

The Purpose of the Temple

The Old Testament **tabernacle was built to house God's presence**:

"And let them make Me a sanctuary, that I may dwell among them." — Exodus 25:8

Yet, by Jesus' time, **religious leaders had turned the temple into a marketplace, distorting its purpose**.

Reflection: Are You Guarding Your Temple?

- Have you allowed **worldly influences** to pollute your faith?
- Do you prioritize **God's presence**, or are distractions taking over?
- Are you ready to **cleanse your heart and walk in full surrender**?

Prayer

Lord, remove anything that dishonors Your presence. Teach me to guard my temple, that my life may remain pure and set apart for You. Father, help me to operate in bold faith and not allow the distractions or desires of this wicked world to deter, dishonor, or distance me from You. Deliver me from any appetite for things or people that lead to destruction, and instead develop in me desires that carry me deeper into Your presence and keep me aligned with Your will. Give me wisdom to guard the gates of my ears and eyes from anything that would water down my faith or contaminate my understanding of Your Word. Help me, Father, to have a sound mind and an alert spirit in this hour. In Jesus' name, Amen.

Day Thirty: When Hell Breaks Loose, Heaven Shows Up!

Scripture: Exodus 5:22-23 & Exodus 6:1-13 (NKJV),
"So Moses returned to the LORD and said, "Lord, why have You brought trouble on this People? Why is it You have sent me?" — Exodus 5:22

"Then Moses returned to the Lord and said, 'Lord, why have You brought trouble on this people? Why is it You have sent me?'" — **Exodus 5:22 (NKJV)**

Introduction- In this passage, **Moses finds himself crying out to God during a crisis that was orchestrated by Heaven.**

Though Moses had obeyed the Lord and returned to Egypt, He **was met with resistance, difficulty, and unexpected pressure.** The deliverance of God's people **would not come easily.** Moses had to learn **that God often uses adversity to strengthen our faith.**

Sometimes, **God hardens the heart of the enemy not to defeat us, but to develop us.** The Israelites had spent **430 years in bondage**, and Pharaoh had grown accustomed to exercising **complete control over them.** But Heaven had arrived **to disrupt Hell's agenda**, even though **Moses did not understand the full plan.**

God's Power in Crisis

Moses was **initially with the plan of God**, until the **pressure of opposition** caused him to **question his calling:**

"For since I came to Pharaoh to speak in Your name, he has done evil to this people; neither have You delivered Your people at all." — **Exodus 5:23 (NKJV)**

Like Moses, many **trust God in the beginning**, but **when adversity strikes, doubt and fear creep in**. We begin to say:

- *Lord, why is this taking so long?*
- *God, did You send me here?*
- *Why does it feel like things are getting worse instead of better?*

But here's the truth: **God does His best work in our worst situations.**

Bondage vs. Breakthrough

The Israelites had been **oppressed for centuries,** accustomed to **slavery and hardship.**

Instead of the Israelites **crying out to God,** they **complained to Pharaoh,** trying to find relief **from the very one who was holding them captive.**

"Then they said to them, 'Let the Lord look on you and judge, because you have made us abhorrent in the sight of Pharaoh...'" — **Exodus 5:21 (NKJV)**

Some believers today remain **bound in toxic situations, addictions, or cycles of defeat** because they seek relief **from worldly sources rather than turning to God.**

Bondage comes in **many forms:**

- **Addictions**—drugs, alcohol, unhealthy relationships.
- **Fear & doubt**—allowing negativity to **override faith**.
- **Worldly dependence**—trusting in success, money, or status rather than **God's provision**.

Yet, **when hell breaks loose in your life, Heaven is already preparing your breakthrough**.

The Lord's Response to Moses

God does **not rebuke Moses for questioning**—instead, He **reminds him of His divine authority**:

"Now you shall see what I will do to Pharaoh. For with a strong hand he will let them go, and with a strong hand he will drive them out of his land." — **Exodus 6:1 (NKJV)**

The Lord reassures Moses that **Pharaoh's oppression is temporary;** deliverance **is coming**. When Heaven moves, **nothing can stand against it**.

Lessons for the Believer

1. **God is with you—even when the process feels unbearable** (Deuteronomy 31:6).
2. **Breakthrough requires endurance—deliverance does not always happen instantly** (Romans 5:3-4).
3. **Bondage ends when we trust God's plan, not when we seek earthly solutions** (Isaiah 55:8-9).

Reflection: Are You Trusting God or Questioning His Plan?

- Are you **seeking relief from the world**, or are you **crying out to God for deliverance**?
- When adversity comes, do you **stand firm in faith**, or do you **begin to doubt your calling**?
- Is the **pressure you are feeling today strengthening your faith** or **causing you to step back**?

Prayer:

Lord, help me to trust Your timing even when the pressure increases. Strengthen my faith to endure adversity, knowing that You are working behind the scenes for my deliverance. Let me lean on Your power rather than earthly solutions. In Jesus' name, Amen.

Day 31-34:

Battling Worry

Day Thirty-One: Overcoming the Trap of Worry

Scripture: Matthew 6:33 (NKJV) *"But seek first the kingdom of God and His righteousness, and all these things shall be added to you."*

Introduction- Jesus reminds us that **worry leads to instability, confusion, and spiritual distraction,** pulling believers away from **faith and into fear.**

He calls us to **seek first the Kingdom**, trusting that He will provide everything we need, instead of being consumed by **temporary concerns.**

The Trap of Worry

Worry is more than **an emotion**—it is a **spiritual attack on trust**:

- It **divides faith**, creating doubt.
- It **pulls the mind** in conflicting directions.
- It **destabilizes the connection** to God.
- It **reveals a lack** of Kingdom pursuit.

"Seek the LORD and His strength; seek His face evermore!"
— Psalm 105:4

Worry consumes our thoughts, then it disconnects us from the **Kingdom** mindset, **wisdom, and inheritance.**

Reflection: Are You Truly Trusting God?

- Do you let **worry interfere with your faith**?
- Are you **mentally consumed by earthly concerns**, or are you prioritizing **Kingdom truths**?
- What steps can you take today to **fully trust in God's provision**?

Prayer

Lord, free me from the trap of worry. Strengthen me to trust You fully, knowing You will provide all I need. Help me focus on Your Kingdom first, walking in peace and faith. In Jesus' name, Amen.

Day Thirty-Two: Are You Listening or Panicking?

Scripture: Mark 4:40 (NKJV) *"Why are you so fearful? How is it that you have no faith?"*

Introduction- Jesus spent time **teaching His disciples,** preparing them to **activate their faith** in moments of difficulty. Yet, when the storm came, **fear overtook them.**

"Teacher, do You not care that we are perishing?" — Mark 4:38

Even after hearing **Jesus' words,** they **reacted with doubt** instead of **standing on faith.** Many believers struggle in the **same way**—knowing **God's truth** but **panicking when trials come.**

Lessons from the Boat

- **Faith Is Built in the Storm** – God allows trials **not to break us, but to strengthen us** (James 1:2-4).
- **Fear Reveals What You Trust** – Do you **believe more in the storm's power than God's authority**? (Psalm 56:3-4).
- **Jesus Sleeps Through What We Panic Over** – He had **peace**, because He knew He had **control** (Isaiah 26:3).

Instead of **whining on the boat**, activate faith **and declare God's promises.**

Reflection: Are You Standing in Faith or Reacting in Fear?

- Are you **applying what you've been taught**, or panicking when trials come?

66

- Do you believe **God is with you**, even in the storm?
- Are you **standing in faith**, or letting **fear control your response**?

Prayer

Lord, strengthen my faith in the midst of the storm. Help me to trust You fully, knowing You hold authority over every situation. Remind me, O God, that it was You who parted the Red Sea, You who rescued the Hebrew Boys, and it is Your name I must call upon in every storm. Father, show me how to rely on You through prayer and the reading of Your Word. Develop within me a belief system that is unbreakable and unshakable. I desire to be closer to You in every area of my life. Help me to mature and grow wise in the storm. Help me to stay the course, anchored in faith. Remind me that I cannot be moved by the storm, but through prayer and the covering of Your righteous Word, I can walk through it victorious. You are my shield and my hedge of protection, O God, and I trust You. In Jesus' Mighty, Matchless Name, Amen.

Day Thirty-Three: Speaking to the Storm

Scripture: Mark 4:39 (NKJV) *"Then He arose and rebuked the wind, and said to the sea, 'Peace, be still!' And the wind ceased and there was a great calm."*

Introduction- Jesus did **not just comfort His disciples—** He **rebuked the storm**. Rather than **talking about the storm**, He **spoke directly to it**.

Many believers spend their **time complaining** about their battles instead of **declaring victory over them**.

How to Survive on the Boat

- **Remember who is with you** – Jesus **is in the storm** with you (Deuteronomy 31:6).
- **Stand on the Word, not emotions** – Let **Scripture guide your response** (Matthew 4:4).
- **Speak to the storm, not about it** – Jesus rebuked the wind, **and it obeyed** (Mark 4:39).

Storms **may come**, but **God has given us the authority** to speak **peace, truth, and victory** in the midst of them.

Reflection: Are You Speaking Life or Complaining?

- Are you **using Scripture to stand firm**, or talking about the storm without declaring victory?
- Are you **trusting God's authority**, knowing that **He has control over every situation**?
- Do you need to **shift your response**, moving from **fear to faith**?

Prayer

Lord, help me declare victory over my battles. Let me stand on Your truth, speak to my circumstances, and trust that Your peace will sustain me. Help me to battle through the bruises, O God. I desire to stand on Your Word and in the truth You've placed within me. Help me to see this battleground as a place of building, not defeat. And if You choose not to move the storm, then stir my spirit and move me within it. Shift my mind from negative thoughts to positive ones. Move me out of fear and mature me to walk fully in faith. Help me to hold on with strength and show me how to wield the authority You have given me through Your Word. Thank You, Lord. In Jesus' name, Amen.

Day Thirty-Four: The Protective Order of Christ

Scripture: Revelation 7:14-17 (NKJV) *"These are the ones who come out of the great tribulation, and washed their robes and made them white in the blood of the Lamb... They shall neither hunger anymore nor thirst anymore... And God will wipe away every tear from their eyes."* — Revelation 7:14,16,17

Introduction- Christ's **protection secures the believer's eternal seat in Heaven**. John describes a **multitude clothed in white robes**, symbolizing redemption through Christ.

This reminds us that God's protection is **not temporary—** it is **eternal security in Him**.

The Promise of Christ's Protection

Scripture declares that those under **His covering** will experience:

- **Robes washed in the blood of the Lamb**— signifying complete redemption (Revelation 7:14).
- **No more hunger or thirst**—indicating full satisfaction in God (Revelation 7:16).
- **Every tear wiped away**—promising divine **restoration and peace** (Revelation 7:17).

But there is also a warning:

"For this reason God will send them strong delusion, that they should believe the lie." — 2 Thessalonians 2:11

Those who **reject Christ** will experience **eternal separation from Him**. Heaven is reserved for **those who**

have surrendered their lives to Him, not just those who claim belief but fail to truly submit.

Reflection: Are You Secure in Christ?

- Have you **fully surrendered to Him**, or are you holding onto earthly distractions?
- Is your **salvation assured**, or are you still resisting His call?
- Are you **covered under Christ's protection**, or are you walking outside of His will?

Prayer

Lord, I submit my life to You completely. Wash me in Your blood, purify my heart, and secure my place in Your Kingdom. Remove distractions that pull me away and let me stand firm in Your truth. In Jesus' name, Amen.

Day 35-41:

The Vision and the Process

Day Thirty-Five: The Picture of Heaven

Scripture: Revelation 7:9 (NKJV) *"After these things I looked, and behold, a great multitude which no one could number, of all nations, tribes, peoples, and tongues, standing before the throne and before the Lamb, clothed with white robes, with palm branches in their hands."*

Introduction- John's vision offers **a glimpse of Heaven's glorious reality**—a **diverse, unified Kingdom**, where believers from **every nation, tribe, and language** worship together.

While different traditions exist within churches today, Heaven is **not separated by culture, race, or denomination**—it is a place of **oneness in Christ**. This passage reminds us that the **Kingdom of God transcends earthly divisions**.

The Kingdom of God is for All Who Believe

The **multitude in Heaven** represents:

- **All nations**—removing the barrier of race.
- **All tribes & tongues**—displaying the vastness of God's creation.
- **All worshipers**—united under the truth of salvation in Christ.

"Salvation belongs to our God who sits on the throne, and to the Lamb!" — Revelation 7:10

This passage reminds us that salvation **is not earned, purchased, or inherited**—it is **a gift from God**, freely given to those who surrender to Him.

Reflection: Are You Living with a Kingdom Mindset?

- Does your **faith reflect unity**, or are you dividing based on earthly standards?
- Have you **fully embraced the truth** that salvation is a gift and not something you must earn?
- How can you **align your worship** with the heart of Heaven?

Prayer

Lord, help me embrace the fullness of Your Kingdom. Let my worship reflect Heaven—uniting in spirit and truth with my brothers and sisters in Christ. In Jesus' name, Amen.

Day Thirty-Six: Sustaining Yourself on Meat, Not Milk

Scripture: Hebrews 5:14 (NKJV) *"But solid food belongs to those who are of full age, that is, those who by reason of use have their senses exercised to discern both good and evil."*

Introduction- Many try to **sustain themselves on spiritual milk**, refusing to **move into maturity**. But a season of **elevation requires depth,** not surface-level faith, but **commitment, understanding, and surrender**.

Milk vs. Meat: What Are You Consuming?

- **Milk:** Surface-level faith, reading but not applying the Word, relying on feel-good teachings rather than deep biblical study.
- **Meat:** Commitment to prayer, fasting, biblical understanding, Kingdom living, and full surrender to God.

"Solid food belongs to those who are mature." — Hebrews 5:14

Shallow faith **cannot sustain breakthrough**—only the **meat of God's Word** can nourish you for **the journey ahead**.

Reflection: Are You Growing Spiritually?

- Are you **operating on spiritual milk**, or have you matured in faith?
- Is your foundation **strong enough to sustain challenges and elevation**?
- How can you **deepen your relationship with God**, ensuring that **your growth is rooted in truth**?

Prayer

Lord, let me feast on the meat of Your Word, growing into full spiritual maturity. Remove every distraction, deepen my wisdom, and strengthen my faith. Lead me into greater understanding, so I may walk fully in Your purpose. Father, do not allow me to grow weary in my walk with You. Instead, mature me in all of my ways. I desire to operate in the full capacity of who You have called me to be. I long to understand the fullness of Your Word and receive divine knowledge and revelation in this hour. Turn my heart and mind away from any childlike habits that hinder growth, development, and understanding. Allow my prayer life to expand. Stretch me in my ability to interpret and absorb Your Word. Do not let a single day pass without me reading Your truth—for I know that within Your Word, I will find You. So have Your way in my life, Lord. I desire to grow and glow—from milk to meat. In Jesus' name, Amen.

Day Thirty-Seven: You Must Be Processed Before You Can Perform

Scripture: Ezekiel 2:1 (NKJV) *"Son of man, stand on your feet, and I will speak to you."*

Introduction- Ezekiel was **called a prophet at age 30**, placed in **an unfamiliar, uncomfortable environment—** yet his assignment remained **unchanged**.

His name means **"God will strengthen,"** confirming his mission would require **divine resilience**.

Before Ezekiel could **step fully into his calling**, he had to first **surrender, submit, and strengthen himself in the Lord**.

Before You Can Perform, You Must Be Processed

God gave Ezekiel a **vision of His throne**, ensuring that he **understood the authority** of the One he was serving:

"Like the appearance of a rainbow in a cloud on a rainy day, so was the appearance of the brightness all around it."
— Ezekiel 1:28

Ezekiel had to:

- **Recognize God's power.**
- **Reverence His presence**.
- **Submit to His authority** before stepping into his prophetic mission.

Have you found yourself **wanting the assignment** but resisting **the process**? Without **spiritual preparation**, the weight of our calling can feel overwhelming.

Reflection: Are You Avoiding the Process?

- Have you **submitted every area of your life to Christ**, or are you still resisting His voice?
- Are you **embracing growth**, or avoiding **the preparation needed for your calling**?
- How can you **deepen your surrender**, ensuring you are **strengthened for your assignment**?

Prayer

Lord, process me for the calling You have placed upon my life. Strengthen me to trust Your authority, embrace Your vision, and walk fully in obedience. In Jesus' name, Amen.

Day Thirty-Eight: The Heart of a Servant

Scripture: Mark 10:45 (NKJV) *"For even the Son of Man did not come to be served, but to serve, and to give His life a ransom for many."*

Introduction- Isaiah **prophesied about Christ**, declaring that He would **establish justice, release captives, and bring light to the nations**.

Jesus did not **come seeking status**—He came **to serve, sacrifice, and fulfill the Father's will**.

The greatest calling of a believer is **not recognition, but servanthood**.

Understanding Servanthood

A **servant voluntarily chooses to serve another**—it is **a calling, not an obligation**.

True servitude requires:

- **Laying down personal desires** – Jesus did not seek **status or approval**, but fulfilled His mission with humility (John 10:14-17).
- **Sacrificial living** – A servant does not place **themselves first**, but prioritizes **God's will and the needs of others** (Philippians 2:3-4).
- **Gratitude in service** – Serving produces a **thankful heart**, aligning us with Christ's nature (Romans 1:8-10).

We are not merely called to **be believers**—we are called to **be servants**.

Reflection: Are You Living to Serve or Seeking to Be Served?

- Are you **seeking status**, or are you **pursuing the heart of servanthood**?
- Do your actions **reflect Christ's humility**, or are they **self-focused**?
- Are you **embracing servanthood with gratitude**, or avoiding the responsibilities of your calling?

Prayer

Lord, teach me the heart of servanthood. Let me walk in humility, submitting to Your will above my own. Remove selfish desires and allow me to serve with integrity and gratitude. In Jesus' name, Amen.

Day Thirty-Nine: Walking in the Calling of a Servant

Scripture: Isaiah 42:1 (NKJV) *"Behold! My Servant whom I uphold, My Elect One in whom My soul delights! I have put My Spirit upon Him; He will bring forth justice to the Gentiles."*

Introduction- Jesus was **appointed by God**, filled with **His Spirit**, and sent on **a divine mission**. His purpose was **not self-seeking but Kingdom-driven**.

If we are to reflect Christ, we must **embrace the calling of a servant**.

The Servant's Calling

Jesus did not use **His position for personal gain**—He **humbled Himself and fulfilled His assignment**:

"The LORD is well pleased for His righteousness' sake; He will exalt the law and make it honorable." — Isaiah 42:21

Walking in servanthood means:

- **Serving in humility** – True leaders serve **without seeking recognition**.
- **Remaining obedient** – A servant listens **to God's voice and follows His direction**.
- **Lifting others** – Servants **strengthen and equip others**, rather than chasing influence.

When we **live as servants**, we step into a **greater Kingdom purpose**.

Reflection: Are You Walking in Servanthood?

- Do you live with **humility**, or are you **seeking validation**?
- Are you **obedient to God's call**, or hesitant to embrace servanthood?
- How can you **strengthen and uplift others**, following Christ's example?

Prayer

Lord, let my heart be aligned with Yours. Help me to serve faithfully, live with humility, and fully embrace the call You've placed upon my life. Remind me that I am fearfully and wonderfully made, and let Your covering of humility rest upon my words, thoughts, and ways each day. I desire to mature in obedience and ask that You teach me like never before. Let my life be an example of Christ in every moment I live. May my actions and conversations reflect how good, gracious, and great You've been to me. Father, let my life be a living sacrifice—one that trusts and yields completely to You. Let my story become a testimony that helps someone else restore their life unto You. Create in me a clean heart, and use me in whatever way You see fit.
In Jesus' name, Amen.

Day Forty: The Dangers of Seeking Elevation Without Process

Scripture: 2 Kings 2:14 (NKJV) *"Then he took the mantle of Elijah that had fallen from him, and struck the water, and said, 'Where is the Lord God of Elijah?' And when he also had struck the water, it was divided this way and that; and Elisha crossed over."*

Introduction- Elisha understood the **cost of the mantle**.

His **first action** after receiving Elijah's anointing was to **call upon God,** recognizing that **without God's presence, the mantle had no power.**

Many individuals **chase titles, positions, and influence** before surrendering **to the process.** But **an unprocessed anointing** leaves us **vulnerable to spiritual attack.**

Examples of Misguided Elevation

- **Adonijah self-proclaimed himself as king**—yet **he was never chosen by God** (1 Kings 1:5).
- **Elisha honored the process**—he sought **God first,** rather than assuming power on his own (2 Kings 2:14).

Just because someone is **anointed** doesn't mean they are **processed. Wisdom, obedience, and character refinement** come before elevation.

Reflection: Are You Prepared for the Next Level?

- Have you **surrendered to the process**, or are you **seeking shortcuts**?

- Are you asking for **God's presence**, or **chasing the title**?
- Do you **trust God's timing**, or are you **trying to force elevation prematurely**?

Prayer

Lord, help me embrace the process before the promotion. Teach me to walk in obedience and preparation, so I may be spiritually ready for elevation. Search my heart, motives, and ways—high and low—to ensure that my character aligns with Your will and Your way. Help me remain rooted in the mindset that it is a privilege to serve You and Your Kingdom. Allow me to seek and pursue You in all that I do, operating under the authority of Your name. Guard me from developing a spirit of platform; instead, posture me in purpose. Help me remain wise, obedient, and focused on refining my character in all things. I trust You with my life and my development. Press me, purge me, and shape me however You see fit. In Jesus' name, Amen.

Day Forty-One: Preparation for Elevation

Scripture: Joshua 1:10-11 (NKJV) *"Then Joshua commanded the officers of the people, saying, 'Prepare provisions for yourselves, for within three days you will cross over this Jordan, to go in to possess the land which the LORD your God is giving you to possess.'"* — Joshua 1:10, 11

Introduction- Joshua was **about to step into elevation,** but God required **spiritual preparation before possession.**

Many **want the blessing,** but few embrace **the refining process** needed to sustain it.

Lessons from Joshua's Commissioning

- **Spiritual Armor Must Remain On** – God's Word **is the armor** and must be meditated on **daily** (Joshua 1:8).
- **Immediate Obedience Is Non-Negotiable** – Joshua **responded without hesitation** (Joshua 1:10). **Delayed obedience is still disobedience.**
- **Preparation Is Key to Elevation** – Before crossing over, Joshua commanded **the people to prepare** (Joshua 1:11). **You cannot carry old habits into new seasons.**

Reflection: Are You Spiritually Prepared for Elevation?

- Are you **fully surrendered to obedience,** or are you **hesitating** on God's instructions?
- Have you **removed distractions,** ensuring you're **ready for the next season**?
- Are you **taking action in faith,** trusting that God **will establish you in His timing**?

Prayer

Lord, prepare me for the elevation You have ordained.
Teach me to walk in obedience. Remove worldly
distractions and deepen my commitment to Your process.
Build within me a confidence that no man or woman can
tear down. Allow me to walk in power and boldness
wherever my feet may tread. Help me to rely fully and
completely on You, O God. Grant me patience and
understanding of Your Kairos and Chronos timing. I know
Your ways are not my ways, and Your thoughts are higher
than mine. Help me to recognize that my harvest is near
and prepare myself to walk into Your promise. I trust You
with my life, Lord, and I trust Your timing. Do not allow
me to enter any place You've destined for me unless my
character and maturity are aligned for the assignment. Help
me to take my time to develop. Break and destroy any yoke
that places unnecessary burdens or delays on my destiny. I
trust You in and out of season, O God. In Jesus' name,
Amen.

Day 42-46:

The Spirit Brings Freedom

Day Forty-Two: Walking in the Spirit, Not the Flesh

Scripture: Romans 6:16 (NKJV) *"Do you not know that to whom you present yourselves slaves to obey, you are that one's slaves whom you obey, whether of sin leading to death, or of obedience leading to righteousness?"*

Introduction- Apostle Paul reminds believers that their actions determine their spiritual condition.

Sin enslaves, but Christ emancipates, calling us to walk in freedom, not return to bondage.

The Spirit responds to how we walk—if we walk in the flesh, we shall reap corruption; if we walk in obedience, we reap righteousness.

How Sin Influences Your Walk

Paul describes how sin attacks believers in three primary ways:

The Lust of the Flesh – Sin tempts believers to satisfy desires outside of God's will (Galatians 5:16-21).

The Lust of the Eyes – Many trust what looks good, ignoring spiritual truth (Genesis 3:6).

The Pride of Life – Pride convinces believers they don't need God, leading to spiritual destruction (Proverbs 16:18).

Our daily choices determine whether we are feeding the Spirit or feeding the flesh.

Reflection: Are You Guarding Your Walk?

- Do your decisions reflect obedience, or are they self-indulgent?
- Are you relying on God's wisdom, or trusting only what looks good?
- Have you crucified pride, ensuring God remains the foundation of your life?

Prayer

Lord, teach me to reject the desires of the flesh, the temptations of the eyes, and the pride that leads to destruction. Strengthen me to follow Your Spirit completely, knowing that true freedom comes from obedience. In Jesus' name, Amen.

Day Forty-Three: Walking in Spiritual Freedom

Scripture: Romans 6:22 (NKJV) *"But now having been set free from sin, and having become slaves of God, you have your fruit to holiness, and the end, everlasting life."*

Introduction- Paul warns believers not to return to sinful habits—true freedom is found in walking in obedience.

Many believers experience deliverance, but fail to maintain their freedom due to distractions, temptation, and spiritual complacency.

The Danger of Returning to Bondage

Adonijah self-proclaimed himself as king, yet he was never chosen by God (1 Kings 1:5).

Elisha understood the cost of the mantle—he asked, "Where is the Lord God of Elijah?" before striking the water (2 Kings 2:14).

A calling without covering leaves you vulnerable—wisdom, obedience, and preparation must come before elevation.

Many fall back into old patterns simply because they fail to guard their walk.

How to Remain in Spiritual Freedom

Daily surrender – Walking with God requires intentional obedience (James 4:7).

Guarding your influences – What you consume affects your spiritual condition (Psalm 1:1-2).

Seeking the Spirit's direction – When you prioritize God's voice, His presence guides your decisions (Proverbs 3:5-6).

Reflection: Are You Walking in Freedom or Falling Back?

- Have you truly embraced spiritual freedom, or are you returning to old habits?
- Are you guarding your influences, ensuring nothing compromises your walk with Christ?
- Do you seek God daily, ensuring you remain in alignment with His will?

Prayer

Lord, keep me grounded in unwavering obedience and complete surrender. Help me walk boldly in spiritual freedom, never returning to the bondage of compromise or confusion. Father, I thank You for delivering me from every place, person, and pattern that has hindered me from experiencing the fullness of relationship with You. I recognize that I am Chosen, set apart, and called according to Your divine purpose. Keep me free from every trap, tactic, and hand of the enemy. Grant me supernatural wisdom and understanding like Elisha, that I may discern, walk in power, and see clearly beyond what's visible. Father, I thank You for keeping Your hand upon my life— protecting my mantle, preserving my calling, and positioning me to move with authority. In Jesus' mighty name, Amen.

Day Forty-Four: Rejecting Compromise and Restoring Holiness

Scripture: Revelation 3:16 (NKJV) *"So then, because you are lukewarm, and neither cold nor hot, I will vomit you out of My mouth."*

Introduction- Jesus **warned against lukewarm faith,** declaring that **halfhearted commitment leads to rejection.**

God calls for us as believers to **fully surrender,** rejecting **compromise and distraction,** to **walk in righteousness.**

Lessons from Jesus' Cleansing of the Temple

- **The Temple Is a Place of Worship, Not Profit** – It should be **dedicated to God's presence**, not **self-serving interests** (John 2:16).
- **Compromise Corrupts Holiness** – Mixing **worldly practices** with sacred spaces leads to **spiritual decay** (Revelation 3:15-18).
- **Lukewarm Faith Leads to Rejection** – Jesus warned that **partial obedience is not enough** (Revelation 3:16).

How to Cleanse Your Spiritual Temple

- **Remove distractions** – Align your heart and actions **with God's will** (Romans 12:2).
- **Reject compromise** – Be **fully committed** to righteousness (James 1:22).
- **Return to true worship** – Seek God **wholeheartedly**, honoring His presence (Psalm 100:4).

Reflection: Are You Living in Full Obedience?

- Is your **faith unwavering**, or have you allowed **compromise to weaken your spiritual walk**?
- Do you need to **repent and recommit** to full surrender?
- How can you **remove distractions and realign with God's purpose**?

Prayer

Lord, cleanse me from lukewarm faith and compromise. Strengthen me to walk in holiness, rejecting distractions that pull me away from You. Let my worship be pure, my actions be righteous, and my heart be fully surrendered. In Jesus' name, Amen.

Day Forty-Five: Walking in the Power of the Holy Spirit

Scripture: Acts 19:6 (NKJV) *"And when Paul had laid hands on them, the Holy Spirit came upon them, and they spoke with tongues and prophesied."*

Introduction- Apostle Paul encountered **12 disciples** in Ephesus who had **received salvation** but **had not yet experienced the fullness of the Spirit**.

Many believers today **accept Christ**, yet they have not fully **embraced the Holy Spirit's presence, power, and transformation. Salvation is the beginning,** but **the Spirit is the empowerment** for the journey ahead.

The Role of the Holy Spirit

"The Spirit of the Lord shall rest upon Him, the Spirit of wisdom and understanding, the Spirit of counsel and might, the Spirit of knowledge and of the fear of the Lord." — Isaiah 11:2

When the Holy Spirit rests upon a believer, they walk in:

- **A new dimension of faith**—confidence in God's authority.
- **A transformed mindset**—rejecting doubt and confusion.
- **Deep obedience**—moving in alignment with God's will rather than emotions.

The Spirit **strengthens, equips, and empowers believers** to complete the assignments placed before them.

Reflection: Are You Walking in the Power of the Holy Spirit?

- Are you **bold in faith**, or hesitant in doubt?
- Have you **received Christ**, but still resist full surrender?
- Are you **drinking deeply of God's presence**, or only sipping at His Word?

Prayer

Lord, I desire the fullness of Your presence. Let the Holy Spirit rest upon me, guiding me into deeper wisdom, faith, and obedience. Remove anything that hinders my spiritual transformation and align my life with Your divine purpose. In Jesus' name, Amen.

Day Forty-Six: Living Fully in the Spirit

Scripture: John 14:15-17 (NKJV) *"If you love Me, keep My commandments. And I will pray the Father, and He will give you another Helper, that He may abide with you forever—the Spirit of truth..."*

Introduction- Receiving the Holy Spirit means **embracing the full lifestyle of Christ**, not merely **claiming His name**.

Many profess faith, yet they **lack the daily intimacy with the Spirit** that transforms their lives.

Living in the Spirit

When believers walk fully in the Spirit, they experience:

- **True peace replacing anxiety** (Philippians 4:7).
- **Faith overriding fear** (2 Timothy 1:7).
- **Obedience becoming priority** (John 14:15-17).
- **Wisdom and discernment sharpening** (1 Corinthians 2:10-12).

The Spirit leads believers into **supernatural encounters, divine purpose, and true transformation**.

Reflection: Have You Fully Embraced the Spirit?

- Are you **living in obedience** or **struggling with surrender**?
- Do you allow **the Spirit to lead**, or are you **operating in your own strength**?
- How can you **deepen your relationship with the Holy Spirit** today?

Prayer

Lord, help me walk fully in the Spirit. Teach me to dwell in Your presence, to grow in wisdom, and to remain obedient to Your divine calling. Father, I long for true peace—a peace that surpasses understanding. Strengthen my faith until it moves mountains and uproots every doubt. Sharpen my discernment and awaken my understanding for the times we are in. I hunger for supernatural encounters with You, O Lord. Reveal Yourself to me in power, in truth, in glory, and in love. I commit myself to the complete lifestyle and character of Jesus Christ. Mold me, shape me, and have Your way in every corner of my life. Do what only You can do. Move, transform, and pour out Your Spirit. In Jesus' mighty name, Amen.

Day 47-49:

The Bold Ask

Day Forty-Seven: Are You Careful in Your Asking?

Scripture: 2 Kings 2:6-15 (NKJV), *"Then Elijah said to him, "Stay here, please, for the LORD has sent me on to the Jordan."* 2 Kings 2:6

Introduction- In this passage, **Elijah** is preparing to leave this world, and **Elisha** stays close, knowing that his time with his mentor is limited.

Before Elijah is taken up, he offers Elisha an opportunity to ask for **one final request**—Elisha boldly asks for a **double portion of his spirit**.

Elijah responds, **"You have asked a hard thing."** Why? Because **true anointing comes with a price**, responsibility, and a call to **faithful stewardship**.

Elisha understood that he wasn't just asking for position— he was asking for the supernatural **power and presence of God** to sustain his assignment.

Be Careful What You Ask For

Many people ask for **elevation, influence, or power**, but fail to consider:

- **Did God call me to this?**
- **Am I spiritually prepared for the responsibility?**
- **Am I walking in obedience and consistency?**

- **Is my request aligned with God's will, or just my desires?**

Elisha wasn't asking for status—he was asking for **the ability to continue the work of the Lord**.

In contrast, **Adonijah in 1 Kings 1:5 exalted himself**, declaring, *"I will be king,"* though he was never appointed. His lust for power led to destruction, while **Elisha's humility positioned him for divine inheritance**.

Reflection: Are You Asking in Alignment?

- Are you asking for **anointing without surrender**?
- Are you pursuing **purpose or personal ambition**?
- Have you allowed **God to process you**, or are you rushing forward **without preparation**?

God does not bless **what is self-appointed—He blesses what is surrendered.**

Prayer

Father, refine my heart so that my asking aligns with Your will. Teach me to honor the process before the promotion, and to seek You first before seeking elevation. Strengthen me to steward well what You have entrusted me with and remove any desires that do not come from You. May my pursuit be after Your presence, not just power. Let me be processed, prepared, and positioned for purpose. In Jesus' name, Amen.

Day Forty-Eight: Asking with Wisdom, Not Ambition

Scripture: 2 Kings 2:9 (NKJV) *"Elisha said, 'Please let a double portion of your spirit be upon me.'"*

Introduction- Elisha could have **asked for status, riches, or recognition**, yet his request was **spiritually sound**—he desired a **double portion** of **Elijah's anointing**.

Many believers **pray for elevation** without realizing the **weight of the calling** they seek. A request **without preparation** can lead to **spiritual struggle instead of success**.

Lessons from Elisha's Request

- **A Divine Calling Comes with a Set Time** – God had already **ordained Elisha** as Elijah's successor (1 Kings 19:16). What God **calls forth**, He establishes in **due season**—we don't have to force it.
- **Honor Unlocks Anointing** – Elisha refused to **leave Elijah's side**, demonstrating **patience, discipline, and humility**. Many today **rush into spiritual positions without preparation**.

True elevation **requires process**—God is more **concerned with preparation than promotion**.

Reflection: Are You Seeking the Right Things?

- Are you asking for **God's presence, or seeking personal gain**?
- Have you allowed **God to refine your character**, or are you trying to step into a calling prematurely?

- Are you **walking in honor and obedience**, or chasing a position without understanding its weight?

Prayer

Lord, teach me to ask with wisdom and humility. Let me seek Your presence above all, not elevation for its own sake—knowing that the anointing is birthed through process. Thank You for reminding me that my calling is divinely timed and ordained from heaven. I desire to seek You wholeheartedly—in all my ways and throughout all my days. Refine me, Lord. Develop my character in Spirit and in Truth. Let my life be a reflection of Your glory and my heart a vessel for Your will. In Jesus' mighty name, Amen.

Day Forty-Nine: The Danger of Choosing Based on Appearance

Scripture: Genesis 13:11 (NKJV) *"So Lot chose for himself all the plain of Jordan, and Lot journeyed east. And they separated from each other."*

Introduction- Lot and Abram faced a **pivotal moment—** they had to **choose where to reside**. Lot picked **based on appearance**, while Abram **chose based on divine direction**.

Lot's decision looked **prosperous**, but it was **spiritually dangerous**. His choice reminds us that **where we settle— physically, emotionally, or spiritually—can shape our destiny**.

Lessons from Lot's Choice

- **Consult God Before Making Life-Altering Moves** – Lot **did not seek God**, while Abram **chose to reside where God was** (Genesis 13:18).
- **Compromise Leads to Spiritual Vulnerability** – Lot first **dwelled near Sodom** (Genesis 13:12), then **moved into the heart of wickedness** (Genesis 14).
- **What Looks Good May Not Be God** – Just because something **appears prosperous** doesn't mean it's **God-ordained**.

Reflection: Are You Rooted in God's Presence or in Worldly Comfort?

- Are you making **moves without consulting God**?
- Have you **lowered your spiritual standards** in exchange for temporary gain?

- Are there **relationships or environments** you need to separate from for divine alignment?

Prayer

Lord, help me seek Your presence above temporary comfort. Train my heart to value Your voice over appearances, and Your will over convenience. Teach me to choose wisely—consulting You before every life-altering move, just as Abram did, trusting that where You dwell is where I am safe. Protect me from the spirit of compromise that leads to spiritual vulnerability. I will not settle near Sodom—I will not inch toward destruction or entertain what is unholy. Keep me far from environments that threaten my peace, purity, and purpose. Open my eyes to discern that what looks good may not be God. Let me not be lured by prosperity that lacks Your presence. Align me with what is truly ordained from heaven. Father, anchor me in wisdom, elevate my discernment, and prepare my heart for every season You've called me to. I trust You to guide me, correct me, and position me for righteousness. In Jesus' mighty name, Amen.

Day 50-52:

Redirection for Restoration

Day Fifty: Trusting God's "No" for Divine Redirection

Scripture: Acts 16:10 (NKJV) *"Now after he had seen the vision, immediately we sought to go to Macedonia, concluding that the Lord had called us to preach the gospel to them."*

Introduction- Paul, Silas, and Timothy **encountered divine restrictions**, yet each closed door **led to greater purpose**.

Instead of preaching in Asia as Paul had planned, the Holy Spirit **redirected them to Macedonia**, a place **far more impactful than they had first envisioned**.

Many believers **struggle when doors close**, failing to realize that every **"No" from God** is a **setup for something better**.

Go Only Where God Permits

- Paul attempted to enter **Asia** but **was forbidden by the Holy Spirit** (Acts 16:6).
- He tried **Bithynia**, but again **was denied** (Acts 16:7).
- **Not every opportunity is a calling**—seek **divine permission, not personal ambition**.

Reflection: Are You Resisting Closed Doors?

- Have you **fully surrendered your journey to God,** or are you **forcing your own path**?
- Are you **trusting His redirection,** or **struggling with disappointment**?
- How can you **embrace divine guidance** instead of **pursuing comfort over calling**?

Prayer

Lord, help me accept closed doors as Your divine redirection. Strengthen me to trust Your plans, even when I don't understand them. Let me walk in obedience, knowing that Your purpose far exceeds my expectations. In Jesus' name, Amen.

Day Fifty-One: Seeking His Face for Restoration

Scripture: 2 Chronicles 7:14 (NKJV) *"If My people who are called by My name will humble themselves, and pray and seek My face, and turn from their wicked ways..."*

Introduction- Solomon interceded for Israel, acknowledging that **sin leads to captivity**, but **God offers restoration** to those who **seek Him with humility, repentance, and obedience**.

Many believers **struggle with cycles of disobedience**, failing to recognize that **God does not overlook unrepentant hearts**. When we **neglect His presence**, we **invite spiritual captivity**.

The Process of Restoration

- **Humble yourself** – Confess sin and acknowledge your need for God.
- **Pray and repent** – Return to a posture of surrender and dependence.
- **Turn away from wickedness** – Repentance isn't just admitting sin—it's forsaking it completely.

God doesn't just **hear prayers**—He responds when we **seek Him sincerely**.

Reflection: Are You Seeking His Face or Just His Hand?

- Are you **fully surrendering**, or **asking for blessings without repentance**?
- Is your **heart positioned for transformation**, or do you keep returning to old habits?

- Are you **actively pursuing holiness**, or letting complacency take over?

Prayer

Lord, I humble myself before You. Forgive me where I have turned away, and teach me to fully seek Your face. Restore me in Your presence, ensuring that my worship is pure. In Jesus' name, Amen.

Day Fifty-Two: Sweeping Your House to Invite His Glory

Scripture: 2 Chronicles 7:12 (NKJV) *"Then the Lord appeared to Solomon by night, and said to him: 'I have heard your prayer, and have chosen this place for Myself as a house of sacrifice.'"*

Introduction- God responded to Solomon's **intercession** by establishing His **conditions for healing**—He required Israel to **cleanse their hearts** before restoration could take place.

Many believers **desire a breakthrough**, but few prepare **their bodies, which is God's Temple for His presence to dwell**.

How to Sweep Your House for God's Glory

- **Reestablish your home as a place of prayer** – Dedicate **every space** to God's presence.
- **Cleanse your heart from distraction** – Remove anything **competing with devotion to God**.
- **Reignite your commitment** – Live with **discipline, obedience, and accountability**.
- **Honor God in your giving** – Ensure your offerings **align with worship, not obligation**.

A purified house **is one that remains in His presence**.

Reflection: Is Your House Ready for His Glory?

- Have you **fully surrendered to repentance**, or are you **holding onto cycles of sin**?
- Is your **home, heart, and life** truly aligned with God's presence?

- Are you operating on a **worldly mindset**, or **a supernatural perspective**?

Prayer

Lord, sweep through my heart, home, and body—every space You've entrusted to me. Prepare me to become a dwelling place for Your glory. I recognize that many seek breakthrough, but few prepare the temple for Your presence to abide. Today, I surrender every part of me for sanctification. Reestablish my home as a sanctuary of prayer, where every room honors Your Spirit. Cleanse my heart from every distraction, uproot every idol, and remove anything that competes with devotion to You. Reignite my commitment. Teach me to walk with discipline, obedience, and accountability. Teach me to honor You not only in my worship, but in my giving—may my offerings flow from gratitude and reverence, never from obligation. Let Your glory fall like never before. Purify me. Align me. Saturate me. May my life remain in Your presence, and may breakthrough manifest because I have made room for You. In Jesus' mighty name, Amen.

Day 53-57:

Obedience Leads to Trust

Day Fifty-Three: Moving with Purpose, Not Just Motion

Scripture: Joshua 1:7 (NKJV) *"Only be strong and very courageous, that you may observe to do according to all the law which Moses My servant commanded you."*

Introduction- Joshua was **called to lead**, but his assignment required more than **movement**—it required **transformation**.

Many believers **go along for the journey**, but never truly **allow God to refine them** in the process.

Just because you're **headed in the right direction** doesn't mean you're **spiritually prepared** for elevation.

Transformation vs. Motion

- **Moving in the right direction doesn't guarantee spiritual growth.**
- **Possession without preparation leads to downfall.**
- **Transformation changes how you think, walk, and obey.**

Joshua wasn't called to **enter the land**—he was called to **occupy it with authority and obedience.**

Reflection: Are You Growing or Just Moving?

- Are you **actively being transformed**, or simply **going through the motions**?
- Do you **prioritize spiritual growth**, or assume elevation will **happen automatically**?
- Are you truly **surrendering to God's process**?

Prayer

Lord, transform me as I journey with You. Strengthen me to walk in full obedience, keeping my spiritual armor secure. Teach me to move with purpose, trusting that Your Word is the foundation of success. In Jesus' name, Amen.

Day Fifty-Four: Obedience Unlocks Miracles

Scripture: Isaiah 1:19 (NKJV) *"If you are willing and obedient, you shall eat the good of the land."*

Introduction- The widow had to **act in obedience before receiving provision**—faith **activates God's promises**.

Are YOU waiting for confirmation, rather than moving in faith?

Yet, true breakthrough comes **not just from belief, but from obedience**.

Dwelling in the Secret Place & Trusting God's Process

- **Dwelling in the Secret Place** – God instructed Elijah to **stay in His presence**, ensuring **supernatural outcomes** (Psalm 91:1).
- **Obedience Leads to Miracles** – Miracles are often **released in faith-filled obedience** rather than hesitation (Isaiah 1:19).

When we **trust and obey**, we position ourselves for **God's supernatural provision**.

Reflection: Are You Walking in Full Obedience?

- Have you **trusted God's Word enough to take action**?
- Are you **waiting for circumstances to change**, or **moving forward in faith**?
- Is your **heart surrendered**, ensuring that obedience leads to breakthrough?

Prayer

Lord, strengthen me to walk in obedience, trusting that You will release Your promises over my life. Let me remain in faith, knowing that miracles come through surrender and action. In Jesus' name, Amen.

Day Fifty-Five: Stop Wavering—Make the Choice

Scripture: 1 Kings 18:21 (NKJV) *"And Elijah came to all the people, and said, 'How long will you falter between two opinions? If the Lord is God, follow Him; but if Baal, follow him.'"*

Introduction- Elijah confronted Israel at **a spiritual crossroads**—they had been **influenced by idolatry**, torn between **God's truth and worldly distractions**.

Many believers today **struggle with divided commitment**, wavering between **faith and fleshly desires**.

God requires **full surrender,** not half-hearted devotion.

Biblical References for Strengthening Your Decision

- **You Cannot Serve Two Masters** – Jesus declared that **divided loyalty is impossible** (Matthew 6:24).
- **The Cost of Following God Requires Full Commitment** – Joshua challenged Israel: **"Choose for yourselves this day whom you will serve"** (Joshua 24:15).

Faith is **not a seasonal choice**—it's a **daily commitment** to God's authority.

Reflection: Have You Fully Committed to God?

- Are you allowing **distractions** to pull you **away from obedience**?
- Are you **relying on your own understanding** or **trusting the move of God**?
- Do you need to **rebuild your altar**, recommitting **fully to God**?

Prayer

Lord, today I choose You without reservation. Strengthen me to resist the pull of divided commitment and fleshly desires. I refuse to waver or compromise in my faith, for I know You require full surrender—not half-hearted devotion. Teach me to walk upright before You, anchored in truth and led by the Spirit. Help me remember that I cannot serve two masters; my heart belongs to You alone. Like Joshua, I declare: "As for me and my house, we will serve the Lord." Empower me to trust You beyond circumstances, feelings, or fear—knowing that You respond with power and precision to surrendered lives. Let my obedience reflect my love for You, and my choices reflect my allegiance to Your kingdom. Today, I recommit my heart, my actions, and my future to You. Purify my desires and strengthen my conviction. I choose truth over temptation, purpose over popularity, and surrender over self. In Jesus' mighty name, Amen.

Day Fifty-Six: Trusting God's Supernatural Power

Scripture: 1 Kings 18:38 (NKJV) *"Then the fire of the Lord fell and consumed the burnt sacrifice."*

Introduction- Elijah **did not just call for commitment—** he demonstrated **God's undeniable power.**

He poured **water over the sacrifice**, proving that **faith must trust God beyond natural limitations.**

Many believers **place limits on God's ability**, doubting His promises when circumstances seem impossible. But **obedience positions us for supernatural encounters.**

Lessons from Elijah's Confrontation

- **Faith Must Trust the Power of God Over Natural Limitations – God's promises do not bow to earthly circumstances** (Genesis 18:14).
- **God Answers the Righteous with Fire – Elijah's obedience led to a supernatural display** (1 Kings 18:38).

When believers **fully surrender**, God **demonstrates His power** in ways **we never imagined**.

Reflection: Are You Trusting God Completely?

- Do you believe **God is greater than your current situation**?
- Are you **fully obedient**, ensuring your heart is **aligned for His movement**?
- Have you asked God to **reignite your faith**, removing doubt?

Prayer

Lord, teach me to trust Your supernatural power beyond what I see, feel, or understand. Just as Elijah poured water over the sacrifice, show me how to lean fully into faith—believing that Your promises are not limited by earthly conditions. Break every mindset that places boundaries on Your ability. I refuse to doubt what You've declared simply because my surroundings seem impossible. You are the God of fire, the God of breakthrough, the God who answers the righteous with power. Position me in obedience. Prepare my heart for surrender. Ignite a deeper level of faith within me that invites Your glory to fall. Let Your presence consume everything unlike You, and transform every area of my life. I believe You are doing more than I can ask, imagine, or contain. Burn away fear. Dismantle hesitation. Elevate my expectation. In Jesus' mighty name, Amen.

Day Fifty-Seven: Faith Over Fear in Uncertainty

Scripture: 2 Corinthians 5:7 (NKJV) *"For we walk by faith, not by sight."*

Introduction- Elijah's journey demonstrates how **faith must override reality**—God commands **divine provision even in impossibility**.

The widow's **natural reality suggested death**, but her **obedience unlocked supernatural provision**.

Many believers struggle to **trust God when circumstances look overwhelming**. Yet, faith is **not based on what we see—it is based on what God has spoken**.

Biblical Examples of Overcoming Natural Reality

- **Supernatural Provision Despite Lack** – Elijah and the widow both faced **scarcity**, yet God **multiplied resources** (Philippians 4:19).
- **God's Command Over Your Reality** – Sarah laughed at **the promise of a son**, but God's Word **superseded earthly limitations** (Genesis 18:14).

Just because **reality seems hopeless** does not mean **God is done working**.

Reflection: Are You Trusting God or Your Circumstances?

- Are you **allowing visible circumstances** to dictate your faith?
- Have you **committed to dwelling in God's presence**, or are you **distracted by worldly options**?

- Are you **obeying God's instructions fully**, or hesitating due to doubt?

Prayer

Lord, teach me to trust Your commands more than my circumstances. Strengthen me to dwell in Your presence, rather than chase temporary solutions. Let my faith override fear, and my obedience unlock supernatural provision. In Jesus' name, Amen.

Day 58-61:

The Cost

Day Fifty-Eight: Chasing Christ Is Going to Cost You Something

Scripture: Luke 12:45-53 (NKJV), *"The master of that servant will come on a day when he is not looking for him...."* (Luke 12:46)

Introduction- This passage in **Luke 12** is not about passive belief—it is about **active discipleship**.

Jesus calls His followers to **steward their faith well, endure refinement, and stand boldly for truth**, even when it costs them relationships, comfort, or security.

Jesus was preparing His disciples **for the cost of following Him**. He wanted them to understand that **discipleship requires sacrifice**—it is not merely about believing, but **about surrendering everything for the sake of His Kingdom**.

The Cost of Discipleship

True discipleship **demands bold obedience**, even when it challenges **human logic or societal norms**. Sometimes, the cost is **tangible**, requiring us to leave behind wealth, status, or personal ambition to follow Christ. Other times, it is **spiritual**, requiring us to **lay down pride, selfishness, and comfort**.

Luke 12:48 reminds us: *"To whom much is given, much will be required."*

Every believer has a **responsibility to advance the Kingdom**—not just in words, but in **action, character, and devotion**. The anointing is not **freely handled**—it demands a lifestyle of **consecration, discipline, and relentless pursuit of God's presence**.

Reflection: Are You Ready to Pay the Price?

- Are you **willing to step out of your comfort zone** for Christ?
- Do you **surrender fully**, or are you still holding onto pieces of the world?
- Will you embrace the **refining fire** necessary for true transformation?

Discipleship is not **passive**—it is a call to **die to self, stand in faith, and walk boldly in God's will**.

Prayer

Lord, strengthen my heart to chase after You no matter the cost. Help me embrace the refining fire that shapes me into the vessel You need. Remove any fear, doubt, or distractions that keep me from total surrender. May I walk in boldness, obedience, and unwavering faith, trusting You completely. Let my pursuit of You be intentional, committed, and relentless. In Jesus' name, Amen.

Day Fifty-Nine: You Can't Survive the Assignment Without Surrendering to God

Scripture: Ezekiel 1:25-28 & Ezekiel 2:1-5 (NKJV),
"Like the appearance of a rainbow in a cloud on a rainy day, so was the appearance of the brightness all around it..." (Ezekiel 1:28)

Introduction- Ezekiel, a priest turned prophet, was called by God at the age of **30** to deliver a message in a **rebellious city** during a critical time.

He was taken captive to **Babylon**, placed in a hostile environment where **God was not honored**, yet entrusted with a prophetic assignment.

His call reminds us that **God's assignments are rarely comfortable**. They require faith, obedience, and total surrender. **Ezekiel was sent to a broken people—but first, he had to be prepared.**

The Process Before the Assignment

Before Ezekiel could **step into his calling**, he had to:

- **Encounter the glory of God** to understand who he was serving.
- **Be strengthened spiritually** to withstand opposition.
- **Fully surrender** so that his faith would not waver under pressure.

"Then the Spirit entered me when He spoke to me, and set me on my feet; and I heard Him who spoke to me." (Ezekiel 2:2)

Reflection: Are You Surrendered?

- Are you **resisting your assignment** because it's uncomfortable?
- Have you **fully surrendered** to God, or are you holding onto distractions?
- Are you **seeking His presence**, or trying to move forward **without His power**?

When we surrender, **we gain strength, clarity, and divine authority**. God does not call the **perfect**, He calls the **willing,** but only **those fully surrendered will survive the mission**.

Prayer

Father, I surrender to You completely. Strengthen me for the assignment ahead and prepare my heart to walk in obedience. Remove every fear, distraction, and doubt that keeps me from embracing Your will. Let me seek You daily, trust You fully, and stand boldly in my calling. May my life reflect Your glory. In Jesus' name, Amen.

Day Sixty: The Consequences of Misplaced Connections

Scripture: Isaiah 39:6-7 (NKJV) *"Behold, the days are coming when all that is in your house, and what your fathers have accumulated until this day, shall be carried to Babylon; nothing shall be left; says the LORD."* (Isaiah 39:6)

Introduction- Hezekiah **thought the alliance was beneficial**, yet it led to **future captivity**.

His lack of **discernment and protection** resulted in **the loss of everything entrusted to him**.

We must be careful—**what seems harmless now** could be **disastrous later**.

Lessons from Hezekiah's Mistake

- **Pride Can Lead to Exposure** – Hezekiah **showed off his treasures**, failing to **credit God for his restoration** (Isaiah 39:4). Self-exaltation **opens the door for destruction**.
- **Alignment Determines Your Future** – Improper connections **can delay or derail destiny**.

Many allow **the wrong influences** into their lives, unaware that **access without discernment leads to downfall**.

Reflection: Are Your Relationships Strengthening or Weakening You?

- Are your **associations leading you closer to God**, or pulling you away?
- Have you **given access to people** who **cause harm instead of uplift**?

- Are you **willing to release unhealthy connections**, trusting God for **divine alignment**?

Prayer

Lord, help me protect what You've entrusted to me. Give me discernment to remove any relationships that threaten my purpose. Let my alignments push me toward destiny, never into destruction. In Jesus' name, Amen.

Day Sixty-One: There is Still a Remnant of God's Faithful Few

Scripture: 1 Kings 19:13-18 (NKJV) *"Yet I have reserved seven thousand in Israel, all whose knees have not bowed to Baal, and every mouth that has not kissed him."* (1 Kings 19:18)

Introduction- Elijah had just witnessed **God's fire** consume the altar on **Mount Carmel**, proving Jehovah alone is God.

He stood boldly against false prophets, secured victory, yet found himself **afraid and discouraged** shortly after.

He allowed exhaustion to weaken his spirit, threats to shake his faith, and **fear to silence his victory**. Instead of walking in triumph, Elijah hid in despair. But God did not abandon him—**He asked one simple question:** *"Why are you here?"*

Why Do We Feel Isolated in Faith?

Like Elijah, many believers feel **alone in righteousness**. We see compromise, spiritual decline, and wonder:

"Is anyone still standing for God?"

But **God always preserves a remnant**—a faithful few who will not bow to culture or lose sight of holiness.

• When we don't see others living boldly for Christ, doubt tries to creep in.

• When the world pressures us to conform, standing firm feels exhausting.

• When victories feel followed by opposition, discouragement tempts us to retreat.

But **your faithfulness matters!** Even if you feel alone, **God is working**—and you are part of His remnant!

Reflection: Are You Standing Firm?

- Are you letting **fear silence your faith**?
- Have you convinced yourself that **you are the only one** standing for truth?
- Is God calling you to **lead and encourage others** in their faith?

Prayer

Lord, help me to stand firm when I feel alone in my faith. Remind me that You have a faithful remnant, and I am called to be part of it. Strengthen me to walk boldly, knowing that You are always working—even when I cannot see it. In Jesus' name, Amen.

Day 62-65:

The Clean Up

Day Sixty-Two: Clean Your Temple

Scripture(s): Matthew 21:12-13 & John 2:13-17 (NKJV), *"Then Jesus went into the temple of God and drove out all those who brought and sold in the temple..."* (Matthew 21:12)

Introduction- When Jesus entered the **Temple**, He expected a place of **holiness and prayer**—a sanctuary where God's presence could dwell.

Instead, He found **greed, corruption, and dishonor**. With righteous zeal, **He cleansed the Temple**, restoring it to its intended purpose.

But before we critique those who defiled the Temple, **we must examine ourselves**. Have we allowed distractions, worldly desires, or self-serving motives to invade **our inner temple**—the place where God wants to dwell within us?

The Purpose of the Temple

In the Old Testament, the **Tabernacle** was God's sacred dwelling place. **Exodus 25:8** declares: *"And let them make Me a sanctuary, that I may dwell among them."*

God designed the Temple with great care because **His presence was meant to abide there**. Yet, by the time Jesus arrived, it had become a place of personal gain rather than **divine revelation and worship**.

The condition of our hearts determines **how we hear from God**.

When our spiritual temple is cluttered with distractions, **it is harder to receive His direction**. But when we **purify our hearts**, we **make room for His presence, wisdom, and intimacy**.

Reflection: Is Your Temple Clean?

- Are distractions, selfish motives, or compromise **keeping you from hearing God**?
- Is your **relationship with Him clouded** by worldly concerns?
- Have you truly **made space for God's presence** to speak and guide you?

When we cleanse our **inner temple**, we unlock **greater revelation, deeper intimacy, and clear direction. A purified heart makes way for divine encounters.**

Prayer

Lord, cleanse my inner temple. Remove all distractions, selfishness, or compromise that would keep me out of Your will and the purpose You have destined for me. Teach me to honor You and seek You with my entire heart—in my worship, in my life, in everything I do. Let me not be lukewarm, but on fire for You. In Jesus' name, Amen.

Day Sixty-Three: Are You Going Along for the Journey or Being Transformed?

Scripture: Joshua 1:7-10 (NKJV), *"This Book of the Law shall not depart from your mouth, but you shall meditate in it day and night…"* (Joshua 1:8)

Introduction- Joshua was called and commissioned by God to take possession of the **promised land**.

Before stepping into his assignment, God gave him **specific instructions**:

"Only be strong and very courageous."

Strength and courage weren't **suggestions**—they were **requirements** to fulfill his destiny. God had already **decreed victory**, but Joshua had to walk in **bold obedience** to possess it.

We must ask ourselves today: **Are we just going along for the journey, or are we allowing God to transform us for the assignment ahead?**

The Transformation Required to Possess the Promise

Every time God speaks **with authority**, transformation must take place. Joshua had to **put on his spiritual armor**, shift his mindset, and move in faith.

We, too, must prepare spiritually when God calls us to something great. **Transformation is required**—we cannot walk in new levels with old habits and half-hearted obedience.

Ephesians 6:11 tells us to: *"Put on the whole armor of God, that you may be able to stand against the wiles of the devil."*

Joshua **wore his armor of faith**, walked in obedience, and **immediately** followed God's instructions. **Delayed obedience is disobedience.**

Reflection: Are You Ready for Transformation?

- Are you merely **going along for the journey**, or allowing **God to transform you**?
- Are you **walking boldly**, or letting **fear delay your obedience**?
- Have you been **wearing your spiritual armor**, or leaving yourself **exposed**?

Transformation requires more than just **movement**—it demands **obedience, discipline, and trust in God's voice**.

Prayer

Father, I surrender my will to Yours. Remove any fear, doubt, or resistance that keeps me from fully walking in my divine purpose. Strengthen my spirit to embrace transformation—shape me into the vessel You need for this season. Equip me with unwavering faith, wisdom, and courage to possess every promise You have spoken over my life. Let my heart be sensitive to Your voice, my steps be ordered by Your word, and my obedience be immediate. In Jesus' name, Amen.

Day Sixty-Four: Are You Under the Protective Order of Christ to Secure Your Seat in Heaven?

Scripture: Revelation 7:9-17 (NKJV), *"They shall neither hunger anymore nor thirst anymore..."*(Revelation 7:16)

Introduction- In this passage, **John the Apostle** receives a divine revelation of Heaven—a place where multitudes from **every nation, tribe, and tongue** stand before God's throne in worship.

Heaven is a place of diversity, unity, and eternal praise, a reflection of what God desires for His Church on earth.

Yet today, many churches remain **segregated, divided, and bound by personal agendas** rather than reflecting the true Kingdom. Jesus did not come to save **one race, one denomination, or one exclusive group**—He came to redeem **all people** willing to accept Him.

A Kingdom Perspective

To fully walk in Kingdom alignment, we must **kill the flesh and build the spirit**—shifting our mindset from earthly limitations to divine understanding. **Salvation is a gift, freely given to those who receive Christ, yet it requires total surrender.**

Revelation 7:9 states: *"After this I looked, and there before me was a great multitude that no one could count, from every nation, tribe, people, and language, standing before the throne and before the Lamb."*

If **Jesus returned today**, would your seat in Heaven be secured? Have you fully surrendered your life, or are you still holding onto **the distractions and comforts of this world**?

The Call to Worship in Unity

True worship is **not about preference—it is about purity**.

Different expressions of worship include:

- **Unified Worship:** The body of Christ standing in agreement, **reflecting Heaven's diversity**.
- **Posture of Reverence:** Just as the elders and angels **bow before the throne**, our worship must reflect humility and surrender.
- **Acknowledging God's Presence:** Worship is **not for entertainment—it is to honor God** and receive divine revelation.

Reflection: Is Your Seat Secured?

- Have you fully surrendered your **life to Christ**?
- Are you **walking in obedience**, or allowing distractions to pull you away?
- Is your **worship pure**, or merely routine?

The Kingdom of God is advancing. The question is: **Are you part of it?**

Prayer

Prayer Lord, I surrender my life completely to You. Let my worship rise not from preference, but from purity. Teach me that true worship is not about sound, style, or sensation—but about spirit and truth. Align my heart with Heaven's order. Help me to walk fully in the center of Your will, never wavering or clinging to what separates me from Your presence. Remove every distraction, fear, and compromise that hinders intimacy with You. Refine me, purify me, and cultivate a spirit that longs for Your glory above all. Position me among the body of believers in unified worship, where Heaven's diversity is honored and Your presence reigns. Help me approach Your throne with reverence, like the elders and angels who bow in surrender. Let my posture reflect humility, and my praise reflect devotion. Worship is not entertainment—it is encounter. Let every moment of praise release revelation, healing, and transformation. Secure my seat in Your Kingdom, O Lord. Let my service be faithful, my obedience unwavering, and my life a living reflection of Your majesty. In Jesus' mighty name, Amen.

Day Sixty-Five: Who You Invite into Your House Will Either Build Your Purpose or Cause You Problems

Scripture: Isaiah 39:1-8 & Isaiah 40:3-5 (NKJV), *"The glory of the LORD shall be revealed, And all flesh shall see it together; For the mouth of the LORD has spoken."* (Isaiah 40:5)

Introduction- In this passage, **King Hezekiah** found himself entangled in both **spiritual warfare and political maneuvering**.

After narrowly escaping death and receiving **15 years of grace from God**, he opened his doors to the **King of Babylon,** an archenemy of the Kingdom.

Instead of standing firm in his faith, **Hezekiah welcomed the visit with excitement**, failing to discern the **hidden motives behind the gestures**. His carelessness would later lead to **loss, captivity, and compromise**.

Be Careful Who You Invite In

Many believers make the mistake of allowing **the wrong people into their spiritual, emotional, and physical space**. Just because someone presents themselves as an ally **does not mean they are assigned by God.**

Consider the dangers Hezekiah ignored:

- **Pleasing the wrong people**: He found **joy** in entertaining **Babylon's representatives**, instead of guarding his faith.
- **Revealing too much**: He **showed them everything in his kingdom**, failing to **recognize the future consequences**.

- **Compromising spiritual authority**: Rather than standing in the **wisdom of God**, he **validated ungodly alliances**.

Reflection: Are You Guarding Your House?

- Are you **careful with who has access to your life**?
- Do you **seek discernment**, or are you **led by emotions**?
- Are you **aligning yourself with the right voices**, or entertaining **spiritual distractions**?

God calls His people to **walk in wisdom,** not **compromise**. Who you allow into your space **will either build or break your purpose**.

Prayer

Lord, help me to guard my heart, my home, and my purpose. Give me discernment to recognize what is from You and what is a distraction. Remove any influences that pull me away from Your will and strengthen my spirit to stand firm in truth. May I seek relationships that edify, sharpen, and align with Your Kingdom, and reject anything that leads to compromise. In Jesus' name, Amen.

Day 66-67:

The Wait

Day Sixty-Six: There is Power in the Wait

Scripture: Acts 1:1-7 (NKJV), *"For John truly baptized with water, but you shall be baptized with the Holy Spirit not many days from now."* (Acts 1:5)

Introduction- In this passage, **Luke**, a physician and devoted follower of Christ, records the transition between Jesus' ministry and the coming movement of the Holy Spirit.

He writes to **Theophilus**, outlining the divine workings of God in the early Church and preparing him for what is about to take place.

Jesus instructs His disciples not to leave Jerusalem but to **wait** for the promise of the Father. Though they were eager to move forward, **they first needed to receive supernatural empowerment**—the baptism of the Holy Spirit.

Their assignment required **patience, faith, and obedience to divine timing**.

The Power in Waiting

Waiting is not **passive—it's preparation.**

Jesus made it clear that without the Holy Spirit, the disciples would **lack the strength and authority** to complete their mission. Likewise, when we **rush ahead without God's direction, we risk stepping outside of His will**.

The benefits of waiting include:

- **Strengthened faith:** Trusting in God's **timing over our own desires**.
- **Spiritual transformation:** Receiving **supernatural wisdom and power** for the journey ahead.
- **Clear direction:** Learning to **move in God's will**, not just in impulse.
- **Heart posture:** Growing in **patience, surrender, and obedience**.

Reflection: Are You Willing to Wait?

- Do you trust that **God's timing is better than your own**?
- Are you moving in **faith, or frustration**?
- Are you allowing God to **prepare you spiritually before stepping forward**?

Waiting **reveals the heart**—those who truly trust **His promise will remain in position until His power is released**.

Prayer

Lord, teach me to wait with faith and patience. Strengthen my spirit to trust Your timing and remain obedient to Your instructions. Remove any fear, doubt, or impatience that tempts me to step ahead without Your presence. Fill me with the Holy Spirit, so that I may walk in wisdom, power, and divine alignment. In Jesus' name, Amen.

Day Sixty-Seven: Jesus Meets You Where You Are

Scripture: John 4:10 (NKJV) *"If you knew the gift of God, and who it is who says to you, 'Give Me a drink,' you would have asked Him, and He would have given you living water."*

Introduction- Jesus **deliberately traveled through Samaria**, choosing to confront **division and brokenness** rather than avoid it.

His encounter with **the Samaritan woman** defied **tradition, social norms, and expectations**, revealing **the depth of His grace**.

She came to the well **looking for water**, but Jesus **offered her something far greater—eternal life.**

Breaking Tradition to Bring Transformation

- Jesus ignored **societal expectations**, choosing to **see her beyond her past.**
- Her **life circumstances led to isolation**, but **Jesus sought renewal, not rejection.**
- God **does not push us away** because of our history—He **meets us to bring healing.**

Reflection: Are You Accepting Jesus' Invitation?

- Are you **allowing Jesus to meet you where you are**, or are you **hiding behind shame**?
- Do you believe **your past disqualifies you**, or are you ready for **grace to transform you**?
- Have you accepted **the living water Jesus offers**, trusting in **His redemption**?

Prayer

Lord, thank You for meeting me right where I am. Just as You passed through Samaria with intention, come into the deepest places of my heart and confront everything that hinders healing. Like the woman at the well, I come thirsty—searching for something deeper. I surrender my past, my shame, and my isolation. Quench my soul with Your living water and lead me into the fullness of eternal life. I choose to step beyond tradition, fear, and brokenness—and walk boldly into Your presence. Restore me. Reposition me. Let my story be a testimony of transformation. I receive Your grace and declare a new beginning. In Jesus' mighty name, Amen.

Day 68-70:

The Fire & Fight is Fixed

Day Sixty-Eight: I Am the Fight for My Prophetic Life

Scripture*: **Psalm 56:1-13 (NKJV)** "When I am afraid, I will trust in You."* (Psalm 56:3)

Introduction – Every believer will encounter seasons where they feel as if they are fighting for their prophetic destiny. David knew what it meant to be pursued—not only by his enemies but by the weight of his divine calling. Despite betrayal, fear, and exhaustion, he never allowed the battle to silence his prayers. Instead, he cried out to God, knowing that intercession was his lifeline.

David's journey teaches us that favor attracts warfare, and that God allows trials as part of our preparation. We cannot step into the fullness of our purpose without being refined in the fire of adversity.

The Reality of Spiritual Battles

• The anointing attracts opposition—David was targeted because he carried divine favor.

• Fear is real, but faith must take precedence—David admitted his distress but placed his trust in God.

• Spiritual battles are not just external; they are internal—God refines His chosen vessels before elevation.

Reflection: Are You Standing Firm in the Fight?

• Have you allowed fear to silence your prayers, or are you pressing deeper into intercession?

• Do you recognize that opposition is confirmation of your anointing?

• Are you trusting God in the fire, knowing that your trial is part of your preparation?

Prayer

Lord, I acknowledge that the battle is real, but I will not retreat in fear. Strengthen my heart and remind me that my trials are refining me for greater purpose. Just as You sustained David, sustain me through the fight for my prophetic life. I place my trust in You and declare victory over every assignment of the enemy. In Jesus' name, Amen.

Day Sixty-Nine: There Is Still a Remnant of God's Faithful Few

Scripture: *1 Kings 19:13-18 (NKJV)* *"Yet I will leave seven thousand in Israel, all the knees that have not bowed to Baal, and every mouth that has not kissed him."* (1 Kings 19:18)

Introduction – After experiencing a great victory against the prophets of Baal, Elijah did not celebrate—he ran. Fear, exhaustion, and isolation made him question his calling. He believed he was the last faithful believer left. But God reminded him that He always preserves a remnant.

Though the world may say faith is fading, though it may seem like believers are few, God has a faithful people who refuse to bow. The cost of standing for God can feel lonely, but victory belongs to those who endure.

Are You Standing as One of the Faithful Few?

• Elijah thought he was alone, but God revealed a remnant—God is always preserving His people.

• The enemy attacks through fear and exhaustion, but we must guard our hearts and minds against deception.

• What the world says does not define the church—God's Word stands forever, and His promises remain unshaken.

Reflection: Will You Stand Firm?

• Do you feel discouraged, believing that faithful believers are few?

• Are you guarding your mind, health, and faith from the attacks of the enemy?

• Will you stay spiritually hydrated—connected to the Word, prayer, worship, and the body of Christ?

Prayer

Lord, when I feel isolated, remind me that I am not alone. You have preserved a remnant, and I choose to stand among them. Strengthen my faith, guard my mind from deception, and renew me when exhaustion threatens my spirit. I will not bow to fear. I will not surrender to discouragement. I declare that I am part of Your faithful few! In Jesus' name, Amen.

Day Seventy: Everything You Need Is in the Fire

Scripture*: **Acts 2:1-8 (NKJV)** "When the Day of Pentecost had fully come, they were all with one accord in one place."* (Acts 2:1)

Introduction – The fire of Pentecost was not just a moment—it was a movement. When the Holy Spirit descended, everything changed. Ordinary men became bold ambassadors of Christ, empowered to preach the Gospel with supernatural authority. The fire activated purpose, unlocked power, and transformed the early church into an unstoppable force.

This same fire is available today. When the Holy Ghost moves, hesitation disappears. Boldness takes over. The fire of God equips, strengthens, and empowers you to fulfill your divine assignment.

Are You Ready for the Fire?

• Spiritual effectiveness requires Holy Ghost fire—God does not call us to operate in fleshly uncertainty.

• Before God moves through you, He must work within you—purging, refining, and preparing you for His purpose.

• Kingdom alignment is necessary—Pentecost required unity before the outpouring.

Reflection: Are You Positioned for Fire?

• Have you surrendered completely to the refining work of the Holy Spirit?

• Are you guarding your mind, heart, and spirit against distractions?

• Are you moving in Kingdom effectiveness or in personal ambition?

Prayer

Lord, ignite me with Your Holy Ghost fire! Cleanse my mind, sanctify my mouth, purify my heart, and discipline my flesh so that I may be used effectively for Your Kingdom. Remove distractions and align me with Your will. I declare that I am ready for the fire—I receive Your power, purpose, and divine activation. In Jesus' name, Amen.

LAST WORDS FROM THE AUTHOR

This 70-day devotional was designed for mature believers, spiritual leaders, and those navigating faith transitions. It offers deep biblical insights and practical applications and challenges readers to move beyond routine faith into active surrender, wisdom, and preparation.

Intended Audience:
- Spiritual leaders & ministers: Seeking guidance on calling, accountability, and leadership.
- Christians in transition: Facing spiritual shifts, new callings, or challenges requiring greater faith.
- Young adults & students: Strengthening their biblical foundation with engaging, relatable truths.

Each Devotional Entry Includes:
- A focused scripture passage connected to the theme.
- A powerful reflection unpacking biblical insights and applications.
- A thought-provoking challenge to align actions with God's will.
- A closing prayer for surrender, obedience, and strength.

This devotional is for those ready to deepen their faith, embrace God's process, and step boldly into His purpose, developing wisdom, discernment, and endurance while remaining faithful to His timing.